HERO

HERO

Rhonda Byrne

ATRIA BOOKS

NEW YORK   LONDON   TORONTO   SYDNEY   NEW DELHI

A Division of Simon & Schuster, Inc.
1230 Avenue of the Americas
New York, NY 10020

The information contained in this book is intended to be educational and not for diagnosis,
prescription, or treatment of any health disorders or as a substitute for financial planning.
This information should not replace consultation with a competent healthcare or financial
professional. The content of this book is intended to be used as an adjunct to a rational and
responsible program prescribed by a healthcare practitioner or financial professional. The
author and publisher are in no way liable for any misuse of the material.

First Atria Books hardcover edition November 2013

ATRIA B O O K S and colophon are trademarks of Simon & Schuster, Inc.

For information about special discounts for bulk purchases, please contact Simon & Schuster
Special Sales at 1-866-506-1949 or business@simonandschuster.com

Artwork concept and art direction by Nic George for Making Good LLC.
Book layout and design by Gozer Media P/L (Australia), www.gozer.com.au, directed by
Making Good LLC.

Excerpt from ILLUSIONS: THE ADVENTURES OF A RELUCTANT MESSIAH by Richard
Bach, copyright © 1977 by Richard Bach and Leslie Parrish-Bach. Used by permission of
Delacorte Press, an imprint of The Random House Publishing Group, a division of Random
House LLC. All rights reserved.

Excerpts from COPY THIS! by Paul Orfalea, copyright © 2005 by The Orfalea Family
Foundation. Used by permission of Workman Publishing Co., Inc., New York. All
rights reserved.

Manufactured in the United States of America

10 9 8 7 6 5 4 3 2 1

Library of Congress Control Number: 2013034709

ISBN: 978-1-4767-5858-9
ISBN: 978-1-4767-5859-6 (ebook)

"Here is a test to find whether your mission on earth is finished. If you're alive, it isn't."

Richard Bach

Illusions

Dedicated to every hero

Acknowledgments

Every new project involves a journey that begins with the seed of an idea and travels its own unique path until its final creation in the world. I love the thrill of the journey, with its unexpected twists and turns, surprises, excitement, and joy. But more than anything else, when I look back on the journey I have taken I am completely humbled by the number of incredible people who played a vital role in helping bring the project into the world. The journey of creating *Hero* was a joy from beginning to end, and I would like to acknowledge the following extraordinary people who made it possible for you to hold this special book in your hands:

Hero's contributors, who came from all over the world to inspire and uplift others through sharing their experiences and whom I had the immense honor and privilege to work with: Liz Murray, Peter Foyo, John Paul DeJoria, Anastasia Soare, Michael Acton Smith, Peter Burwash, Mastin Kipp, G. M. Rao, Pete Carroll, Laird Hamilton, Layne Beachley, and Paul Orfalea. Thank you for trusting in me, for unhesitatingly giving your precious time, and for seeing the vision and potential of *Hero* when it was just a seed of an idea.

The contributor's wonderful assistants for their invaluable help. The amazing people working for the contributors' foundations and charities; thank you for being a part of *Hero* and allowing us to highlight the great work you are doing. Special thanks to Mayra-Alejandra Garcia, Luca Carp, Bhuvana Chakravarthy, Jaime Davern, Megan McGrath, and Tamara Azar.

The Secret team members Skye Byrne and Paul Harrington, who worked closely with me in creating the structure of *Hero,* who undertook the enormous task of compiling the contributors' words, and who provided genius insights throughout its creation. In addition, thanks to Skye, for her depth of understanding and brilliant editing of my writing; *Hero* would not be what it is without her editing.

Glenda Bell, who project managed *Hero,* and who not only brought the contributors to *Hero* but who managed the scheduling of interviews and liaised with all the contributors' foundations, and Andrea Keir, who worked diligently side by side with Glenda to bring the perfect contributors to *Hero*. Thank you.

Jan Child, who is in charge of publishing for The Secret. Thank you for your encouragement, enthusiasm, and tireless work on *Hero* in uniting the publishing, graphics, and website teams from across the planet into a united creative force.

The creative director of The Secret, Nic George. Thank you for your magnificent drawing and original artwork for *Hero,* and for continually inspiring me with my writing to live up to your graphic work. To our graphics team at Gozer Media, Shamus Hoare and Anna Buys, thank you for your dedication and talent yet again.

My phenomenal publishing team at Atria Books and Simon & Schuster for their support of my books, of The Secret, and me. Thank you to Carolyn Reidy, Judith Curr, Dennis Eulau,

Darlene DeLillo, my editor Sarah Branham for her guidance, Lisa Keim, Eileen Ahearn, Paul Olsewski, Jim Thiel, Daniella Wexler, and copyeditors Isolde Sauer and Kimberly Goldstein.

The Secret team members whom I am blessed to work with every day: Donald Zyck, Lori Sharapov, Mark O'Connor, Josh Gold, my personal assistant Jill Nelsen, Cori Johansing, Peter Byrne, Chye Lee, and Marcy Koltun-Crilley.

Our legal team at Greenburg Glusker: Bonnie Eskenazi and Aaron Moss. My eternal thanks to Brad Brian of Munger Tolles. To Laura Reeve and the team at our P.R. company, Edelman, thank you.

My dearest friends and family, who continue to support and inspire me in my work, and whose presence in my life I dearly cherish. Thank you. And to my wonderful parents – you were the absolute best.

My daughter Hayley, who teaches me to ask for answers beyond what is known in the material world, and her perfect creation, Savannah Byrne-Cronin. For their love and support, Kevin "Kid" McKemy, the beautiful Oku Den, Paul Cronin, and Angel Martin Velayos for his continual spiritual guidance and wisdom.

Lastly, the idea for *Hero* came through a flash of insight that I received one evening, and so my deepest gratitude to the Universe and the Universal Mind for inspiring me with such a special project, and for guiding me through every step of its journey to its creation on planet Earth.

Contents

Introduction

This book is about a story. It's a story that changed my life, and throughout history has changed the lives of many other human beings. This story has been told since the beginning of time. It has appeared in different forms in every culture and country of the world, but the essence of the story always remains the same. The story is about a hero who undertakes a courageous journey on planet Earth.

The setting of planet Earth is an exquisitely beautiful one – filled with vast oceans, mountains, jungles, breathtaking coastlines, sweeping plains, and spectacular animals and creatures of every kind – and along with the beauty of the natural world is all of the joy that is experienced by the human beings who inhabit it. But as the hero discovers, life is also very challenging for human beings on earth. Growth is painful, from childhood to adolescence, adulthood, and eventual old age, and there are the experiences

of physical suffering, poverty, and grief, and eventual death
for everyone.

There is both joy and suffering on planet Earth because this
beautiful world is a world of duality – a world of opposites.
There is an opposite side to everything. There's light and there's
darkness, near and far, up and down, left and right, hot and cold,
and these opposites are experienced at every level of life. There
are friends and enemies, falling in love and falling out of love,
security and uncertainty, wealth and poverty, bliss and despair,
and in every human there are positive and negative qualities. On
planet Earth, everything has its opposite.

And it's this world with its equal potential for great joy, great
love, great challenges, and great suffering that you wanted to
come to. It's you who wanted to come here and experience the
adventure of living in such a beautiful but challenging place. It's
you who were determined that there was no difficulty so great it
would stop you from discovering the hero within you. It's you
who wanted to take the Hero's Journey… for you are the hero of
this story.

You are not left unequipped when you undertake the Hero's
Journey. You were born with immensely powerful abilities within
you that would enable you to realize your dreams and overcome
every trial, obstacle, and challenge you would encounter. But
in being born into the limited material world of planet Earth,
your mind and consciousness became limited too, which meant

you wouldn't remember your true nature, and you wouldn't remember the powerful abilities within you. You would have to discover them for yourself.

Only through completing the Hero's Journey and allowing your highest human qualities to arise within you will you finally become the hero. And then a new purpose will overtake your heart – to help those who are beginning their own Hero's Journey, with everything you discovered on the path.

The people you're about to meet have already taken their Hero's Journey. They've come together from all over the world to share their stories and everything they experienced to help you begin your own Hero's Journey.

LIZ MURRAY – FROM THE UNITED STATES OF AMERICA

Liz Murray was born to drug-addicted parents and grew up in poverty in New York City. After her mother died and her father went into a shelter when Liz was a teenager, she found herself homeless. Liz hadn't finished school, was sleeping in stairwells, and shoplifting food to survive, but it was at that time that a dream was born within her to attend Harvard University. Four years later Liz fulfilled her dream, and through sharing her story she has gone on to become a best-selling author and one of the most sought-after motivational speakers in the world.

G. M. RAO – FROM INDIA

G. M. Rao grew up in a small village in India with no electricity and no telephones, where residents had to line up for their quota of supplies. Despite failing his first attempt at his junior high exams, Mr. Rao wanted to go into business so that he could settle down one day with a small business and a nice house. Luckily, he also stayed very open to opportunities that came his way. From his initial business of a jute mill, Mr. Rao gradually expanded his businesses until today his huge empire includes power plants, development of airports and highways, and urban development.

LAIRD HAMILTON – FROM THE UNITED STATES OF AMERICA

Laird Hamilton grew up in a broken home in Hawaii. Feeling excluded and discriminated against and realizing he needed to grow up fast, he set out to prove himself as a surfer and go where no surfer had gone before. His extreme adventures in and out of the water led to many serious injuries, broken bones, and being lost at sea on numerous occasions, yet Laird Hamilton still realized his dream to break the limits of what was possible and went on to become one of the greatest big-wave surfers the world has seen.

ANASTASIA SOARE – FROM ROMANIA

Anastasia Soare and her young family fled Communist Romania at the height of the Cold War, seeking a better life. She arrived in Los Angeles without money or the ability to speak English and worked fourteen-hour days in a beauty salon. When Anastasia realized that nothing was going to change in her life until she changed what she was doing, she decided to start her own business – in Beverly Hills. Anastasia experienced instant success with her unique method of shaping eyebrows, and over the years has turned the art of eyebrow shaping into a national and global empire.

PAUL ORFALEA – FROM THE UNITED STATES OF AMERICA

Paul Orfalea struggled through his school years with severe dyslexia and ADHD. Though essentially unable to read, Paul held the ambition to build a company bigger than IBM. To overcome his literacy challenges Paul developed a keen sense of observation, and while standing in a line one day this skill enabled Paul to see a need – for cheap printing and photocopying. From that one idea, Kinko's was born, which eventually grew into a billion-dollar photocopying company.

PETER BURWASH – FROM CANADA

Peter Burwash was a young ice hockey player when a heavy collision left him lying on the ice with his lower body paralyzed. He vowed that if he walked away from that, he would give up hockey forever. True to his word, when he was able to stand up an hour later, Peter packed his bags and set out to become a tennis professional. While he never became a top-ranking tennis player, Peter did go on to become one of the most revered tennis coaches of all time and to build the largest tennis management company in the world.

MASTIN KIPP – FROM THE UNITED STATES OF AMERICA

Mastin Kipp had the world at his feet as one of the youngest junior executives in the Los Angeles music industry. But an escalating drug and alcohol habit eventually led to the greatest shock of his life; Mastin was fired. After losing everything materially but gaining in wisdom, Mastin set about reinventing himself, and has since become an inspirational blogger and writer through his rapidly growing website, email, and Twitter account, *The Daily Love*.

PETE CARROLL – FROM THE UNITED STATES OF AMERICA

Pete Carroll dreamed of doing only one thing with his life – playing sports and having a career playing professionally. But that dream was cut short when he failed to make the grade in the National Football League. It left Pete with no idea what he would do with his skills or his life – until he realized that his dream could still come true, but in a way he'd never thought of. Pete became a football coach, and although his journey of professional coaching was full of ups and downs, he emerged to become one of the most inspirational American football coaches of all time, and was recently awarded the NFC coach of the year of the Seattle Seahawks.

MICHAEL ACTON SMITH – FROM ENGLAND

After graduating university, Michael Acton Smith found himself virtually unemployable. He decided to go into business, but couldn't raise any financing from the bank, so his mother loaned him £1,000. Several failed enterprises later, he was on the brink of bankruptcy, but Michael knew without a doubt his latest idea was something very special. Sure enough, Moshi Monsters took England by storm, and became a global phenomenon in kids' entertainment.

LAYNE BEACHLEY – FROM AUSTRALIA

Layne Beachley's mother died tragically when she was just seven years of age. Not long afterward, Layne discovered she had been adopted as a baby. Layne dealt with her feelings of loss and abandonment by setting a goal for herself that would prove her worth to the world – become a world-champion surfer. Layne Beachley achieved her goal, winning the world title not once but a record seven times, making her the world's greatest female surfer.

John Paul DeJoria – from the United States of America

John Paul DeJoria and his brother spent four and a half years of their childhood in a foster home because their ill mother could not work and take care of them at the same time. They both ended up in a kids' street gang in East Los Angeles, and a high school teacher predicted John Paul would never amount to anything. When John Paul was in his twenties and he and his infant son were living in a car and John Paul was collecting bottles to survive, it seemed the prediction had come true. But John Paul was determined to make something of his life. After being fired three times in a row, John Paul partnered with Paul Mitchell, and with just $700 they started their own hair-product company. John Paul Mitchell Systems would go on to earn revenues in excess of $1 billion a year.

Peter Foyo – from the United States of America

Peter Foyo was a child of hardworking immigrants to the United States. As a child, he dreamed of a technological future where cities ran on solar power and telephones were mobile. When he got older, he dreamed of having a business so huge and successful that he would be the best executive in Latin America. Anyone would have said these were impossible dreams, but Peter realized his dream when he became president of telecommunications giant Nextel Communications Mexico at just thirty-three years of age.

As for me, I was born into a humble working-class family in Australia. I didn't have any big aspirations in my early years because I didn't think big dreams were possible for me. But in 2004, my life changed forever when I discovered a secret, and a huge dream took over me – to share the secret I had discovered with the world. In 2006, *The Secret* film and book were released, and they swept the globe, reaching tens of millions of people.

If you are like I once was and you've never considered having big dreams because you didn't think they could happen, know that on the journey you're about to take you will discover everything you need to make your dreams – however impossible they may seem – come true.

This is your story. This is your purpose. This is why you are here on planet Earth – to take the Hero's Journey and to discover the hero within you. With the invaluable wisdom you're about to receive, and armed with your powerful abilities, you will be able to fulfill your dream and find the true and lasting happiness that every one of us so desperately seeks. No matter where you are in your life, no matter what age you are, it is never too late to follow your dream.

Part One

THE DREAM

THE CALL

The Call to Adventure

Against All Odds

No one is born into a perfect life. If you were, you wouldn't have anything to strive for, and you wouldn't have the urge to create something with your life. You wouldn't have any dreams at all. Whatever circumstances you were born into, whatever family life and education you had or didn't have, you came here to make your dreams come true, and no matter where you are now, you are fully equipped with everything you need to do it!

ANASTASIA SOARE
FOUNDER – ANASTASIA BEVERLY HILLS

I started from nothing. I really, really started from nothing. We had no money. I didn't speak the language. I had no idea how a Western country worked – the mentality, the financial system. I didn't even know how to write a check, because we didn't have that in Romania. I started literally learning the alphabet.

Paul Orfalea
Founder – Kinko's

Not many kids manage to flunk the second grade, but I did. I couldn't learn the alphabet. I couldn't read. I was always in trouble. I couldn't control myself. I was just so impulsive. I was finally expelled from high school at sixteen.

The tougher the circumstances are in our life and the more the odds are stacked against us, often the more of a catalyst those circumstances will be in propelling us to find our dream.

Peter Foyo
President – Nextel Communications Mexico

My parents were immigrants to the United States, and we started with nothing. I remember having my pants above my ankles. My father was a general in the country he came from, and when he got to the United States he ended up being a chimney sweeper.

Laird Hamilton
Big-Wave Surfer

I grew up in a racially tense environment that had people hating me for how I was born.

"I had all the disadvantages required for success."

Larry Ellison

Cofounder of Oracle Corporation

JOHN PAUL DEJORIA
COFOUNDER – JOHN PAUL MITCHELL SYSTEMS

I was twenty-three years old, and my son was two and a half, and my wife at the time had left. Our rent wasn't paid for three months, so they kicked us out. We ended up sleeping in the car. The way we survived was we would go around collecting soda bottles and cash them in.

From these circumstances as a young adult, it's hard to believe that John Paul DeJoria went on to create the hugely successful hair-product company John Paul Mitchell Systems. John Paul created a life for himself that is unrecognizable from the life he began with, and he did it by using qualities that you have within you now.

G. M. RAO
MECHANICAL ENGINEER, FOUNDER – GMR GROUP

I started with a zero base. My village was small – only 5,000 people. There was no telephone and no power. We had one bottle of iced water that we would share, and we had to line up for our quota of sugar and milk for the month.

Whether you were born in India, Australia, the United States, France, or Singapore, the circumstances of your beginnings do not dictate the kind of life you will lead. There is not a single human strength or quality that you are missing in order to fulfill your dreams. You have everything within you to be or do whatever you want, even if the odds appear to be against you.

PETE CARROLL
NFL COACH – SEATTLE SEAHAWKS

Once I was done playing football in college I tried out for an NFL team and then a World Football League team. But when I got cut for the last time I really was in shock. I had no direction, because everything that I'd ever looked toward was about playing. I was suddenly faced with – what now?

After suffering a life-threatening injury as an ice hockey player, Peter Burwash went on tour playing tennis, despite his lack of professional tennis ranking or tournament success. With no money, he survived mostly on a jar of peanut butter and a two-day-old breadstick, which he divided into pieces to last for five days. After seven years on the tennis circuit, Peter was forced to retire, and once again he found himself in a situation where his chances for success seemed to be little to none.

Peter Burwash
TENNIS COACH, FOUNDER –
PETER BURWASH INTERNATIONAL

*When it came time to form our tennis management company
there were sixteen other companies doing the same thing. I
had the least amount of money, financial backing, and tennis
credibility. We didn't have any chairs in the office, so we had
meetings on the floor for the first couple of years.*

It's not the conditions of the outside world that determine
whether or not your dreams will be fulfilled. It's not how much
money you have, how educated you are, who you know, or even
how much experience you have. It's the discovery of the abilities
you have within you and knowing how to use them to overcome
any and every obstacle you meet in the outside world. It's what
every successful person did, and you can do it too.

Michael Acton Smith
FOUNDER – MIND CANDY

*I had a friend, Tom, who I met at university, and we decided
to set up a business together. We didn't have much money;
in fact, we had debts from university. We got the cash to
get the business going after we saw an ad in a newspaper
asking people to basically sell their bodies to medical science
by taking part in a drug test for a new antimigraine drug.
We did that and got paid £400 each. My mum was horrified.
I think that was one of the reasons why she was very*

supportive. She gave us £1,000 each, and Tom's parents let us use their attic.

Ten years ago I was doing fine in my life, climbing the ladder of success in the television industry, and then suddenly one devastating circumstance after another happened, and within a few short months my entire life had collapsed around me. I fell into despair, but it was in this very moment that I discovered a secret that ultimately would become a movie and my first book. Even when your whole life seems to have burned to the ground, from the ashes comes new life.

MASTIN KIPP
INSPIRATIONAL WRITER, FOUNDER –
THE DAILY LOVE

When I first came to Hollywood I wanted to be a music manager. That didn't really work out – Hollywood's not known for being the most loving environment. I started abusing drugs and alcohol, and I hit rock bottom. In one week my investors pulled out, my business partner and I broke up, my roommate gave me three days' notice, I developed gout in my foot, my lower back went out, and the girl I was seeing, she and I broke up. Literally, my life fell apart in one week. That started a very long and painful journey that I'm very grateful I went on but never want to do again. At the time I felt like I was in a hurricane, and then I realized: What if it was a divine storm?

LIZ MURRAY
HARVARD GRADUATE, AUTHOR AND SPEAKER

I went through this period of time where I had things, and then I suddenly didn't have anything tangible. My mom passed away, my dad was estranged and living in this shelter, and my uncle – who was probably the biggest angel of my life – passed away suddenly. I ended up homeless. Everything that was there was suddenly not there. I remember feeling like, if life can change for the worse maybe life can change for the better, because clearly life could change very quickly.

Life circumstances can be very tough, as they were for Liz Murray, but those circumstances were what provided Liz with a burning desire that took her off the streets of New York City to attend Harvard University. When you find that burning desire to be or do something, you've found a powerful force that can cut through seemingly impossible circumstances and limitations.

By realizing your dreams, you will realize the greatness in you. Greatness is not being born with a silver spoon in your mouth. Following your dreams and realizing the hero within you is greatness.

Your Calling

Every single person who has ever been born or ever will be born comes with some unique talent or ability. It's this special thing about you that is your calling. Although no human being is born without it, many will live their lives without discovering or living their calling.

Your calling is something that moves you like nothing else in life. It's something you're attracted to, something you're passionate about, and it fills you with joy and sets your heart on fire when you do it.

Your particular calling might be a burning desire to achieve something in business, sports, your job, or your career. It might even be your hobby. A hobby can be a clue to your calling, because it's something you're passionate about and that you make the time to pursue. Plenty of people's hobbies have turned into big dreams that became big companies.

MICHAEL ACTON SMITH

The thing I have always loved ever since I was little was games. I loved playing. I think it is a very important part of being human. So my big dream has always been to run a games company, designing games and entertaining people.

PETE CARROLL

Even though I'd coached since the time I was thirteen years old in camps and things like that, I never connected that with something that I would do. When I went back to graduate school I was a coach at the University of the Pacific, and that's when I stepped back and thought, "Well, this is something I could do that's close to playing football." And that's where I really made my first step toward coaching.

Your calling might be something you have daydreamed about being or doing that you thought could never happen for you, but when you think about doing that particular thing and living that life you're filled with an incredible feeling of happiness and fulfillment. And no matter how impossible that dream seems to be, you are being called to follow it.

LIZ MURRAY

I would sleep by myself in a hallway in New York City. I shoplifted Oreos and crackers, and I would sleep with my head on my book bag. In my book bag I had everything I owned – my journal, my clothes, and my mother's picture, which I carried with me everywhere. With my head down on that book bag, sleeping in that hallway, I would dream of a better life. And I had this deep sense inside of me that I was meant to transcend whatever this was, not only for the purpose of having a better life, but for making the lives of others better.

Whether you can remember it or not, you have received the call several times in your life already. You might have received it as a child when you knew absolutely what you wanted to be when you grew up. But then society or well-meaning parents and teachers influence us with the limited options of what we can or can't do, and we shut down our calling and our dreams.

PETER FOYO

Ever since I was a very small boy I was dreaming very big ideas. Long before wireless phones I was dreaming of how neat it would be to have a telephone in my hand that wouldn't have any wires attached. Wouldn't it be amazing if I could put a card inside a gas pump and pump my gas? Wouldn't it be amazing if we could run cities from the sun? I had a vision of creating this great company, making lots of money, and being the best executive in Latin America.

You might have received the call in what seemed like an everyday moment, through something you saw, read, or heard. Suddenly something hit you like a bolt of lightning, and an ordinary moment becomes the defining moment of your life.

G. M. RAO

My mathematics teacher in school said every life has a purpose and we should work toward realizing it because that would be real achievement. This ignited a burning desire in me to seek my calling and work toward achieving it.

LAIRD HAMILTON

My father left my mother when I was very young, and I had to be a little man very early. That forced me to really make a conscious decision that I wanted to be something.

Out of challenging life circumstances, a burning desire arose within Laird Hamilton to do something with his life. He heard the call, he responded to it, and in fulfilling his dream of becoming one of the greatest big-wave surfers, he has inspired millions of people the world over.

For Layne Beachley, the call also came through a very challenging situation in her childhood. When Layne was only seven years old, her mother died suddenly. After her mother's death, Layne learned she was adopted. Her birth mother was only seventeen when Layne was conceived through a date rape.

Layne's foundation crumbled beneath her. But it was that critical event of losing her mother that would propel Australia's Layne Beachley to become one of the greatest female athletes in the world.

LAYNE BEACHLEY
SEVEN-TIME WORLD SURFING CHAMPION

Honestly, what drove me to become a world champion is being adopted. Before I chose surfing, the big dream was to be a world champion in anything. I just had to be the best in the world. I felt the need to prove myself to the world.

PAUL ORFALEA

There was never any doubt in my mind what I wanted for my life. I just wanted to have my own business. Could have been any business. I used to look at the IBM building and think, "I want a business bigger than that."

Suffering from ADHD and dyslexia, Paul Orfalea couldn't read or write, yet look what he did with his life. He created Kinko's, a multibillion-dollar company that provided jobs for thousands of people. In our world of duality, every disadvantage contains its opposite, an advantage; Paul turned his disadvantages into advantages.

Anastasia Soare had a dream of escaping Communist Romania. For almost three years she planned and waited to make her escape with her daughter. Her decision to flee involved great risks, and when she finally arrived in the United States, Anastasia came face to face with another huge decision. She was working fourteen-hour days to earn enough money to support her family, and unless she did something different, this would be her lot in life.

ANASTASIA SOARE

I needed to do something. I needed to prove and to find out who I was as a person, what I was worth. I'm not saying it wasn't scary, because it was scary. But I thought, "This is why I came to this country. This is the land of opportunity.

I have to do this, otherwise why did I come here? To have a worse life than I had in Romania? No."

Living under very difficult circumstances in Romania instilled in Anastasia a particular strength of character, and a determination that would carry her through every obstacle to fulfill her dream of having her own business. That business grew into an empire with over 1,000 outlets in the United States, more than 600 outlets internationally, and salons in multiple countries throughout the world.

No life circumstances are 100 percent negative. Every negative circumstance also contains its opposite, and so there is something good buried within every seemingly bad situation. Life is not about the negative circumstances that happen to you, it's about what you do with the golden opportunities hidden within!

You're never called to follow a dream unless there are multiple ways for you to fulfill it. It's downright impossible for you to have a dream if you can't at the very least make the essence of that dream come true. Your dreams are calling you to the best life you can have; they are calling you to find the hero within you.

MASTIN KIPP

I grew up in a relatively picturesque environment. My parents were awesome, and that did a lot to shelter me from the pain in the world. When I started to step outside myself and see the pain in others and realize that I could do

*something about it, it made it crystal clear that there was
really nothing else I could do with my life. And so my dream
has really been to combine pop culture with inspiration
and wisdom, so that we can reach the greatest number of
people possible.*

If you hear the call and you don't respond to it because you're
too scared or you don't believe you can achieve it, sometimes
circumstances will push you to follow your dream, as
happened with me.

I was working as a television producer at a network, and I used
to dream of starting my own television production company.
I would never have done it because I had a family to support,
my job paid well, and we needed the money to eat and keep a
roof over our heads. I clung to the security of my job with all my
might, despite many people urging me to start my own company.

Then, I got fired. I was in shock. How would we eat? How could
we pay for our daughters' education? How could we pay the
mortgage on our house?

One option I had was to get a job at a different television network.
But I couldn't bear the thought of going back to what I had been
doing. I realized that since I had been fired I had nothing to lose,
and so I started working on ideas for television shows on a plastic
table and chairs in the back room of our very humble house.
I developed an idea and created a pitch for a television show,

even though I had no idea how to create a pitch. But I believed in the idea, and so, with heart pounding and legs trembling, I presented the idea to executives at one of the networks. The show was commissioned on the spot, and when it aired it was a huge success and became a long-running series.

Through being fired I was given the perfect circumstances to finally answer my calling and live my dream, and I remain grateful to this day for that television network firing me. Without them, I would have refused the call to follow my dream, and I would have missed living the most exciting and fulfilling journey of my life.

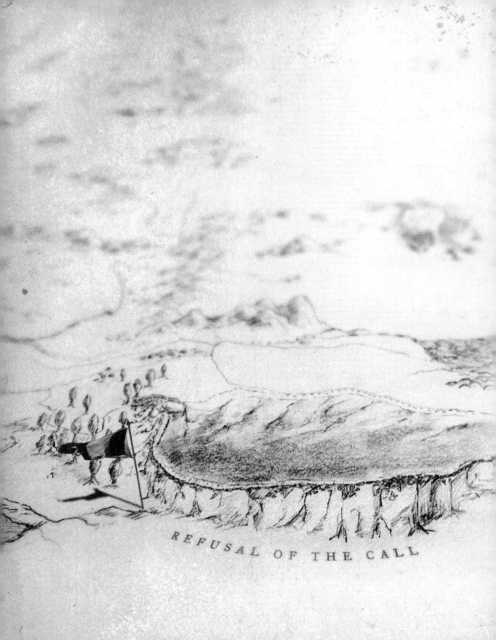

REFUSAL OF THE CALL

Refusal of the Call

LAIRD HAMILTON

The risk that you take in not pursuing your dream is terminal. It's the end. It's a life without fulfillment, it's a life without accomplishment, it's a life without contentment, and it's a life without joy. It's misery.

When you refuse the call from life to follow your dreams, you run the risk of living an unfulfilled and unhappy life. No matter what you do, and no matter what material things you acquire along the way, if you don't do the things that make your heart sing you will feel an overwhelming sense of dissatisfaction and regret when you get to the end of your life. Don't let this be the story of your life. No matter how young or how old you are right now, you have a greater story to live! It may seem like a big risk to follow your dream, but isn't the greatest risk of all to miss your life?

MICHAEL ACTON SMITH
To never give your dreams a chance is the biggest failure.

G. M. RAO
When you don't follow your dream or passion, then what you work for will seem like a cage, albeit a golden one. Body without soul! It will result in being frustrated, listless, and completely devoid of a purpose for existence.

Responding to your calling and deciding to follow your dreams is actually the easy way. Refusing the call is the hard way, because you risk being miserable and dooming yourself to a life without joy, a life without passion, and a life without meaning or purpose.

Perhaps you started out loving your current job, but in time your work has become a grind to you. This might mean your current job is not your ultimate calling, and you need to dig deep and ask yourself whether somewhere along the way you put your dreams aside.

LAYNE BEACHLEY
If you're doing anything in life that's not making your heart sing, that's not fueling your passion to get up on a daily basis, then you're not fulfilling your role as a human being on this planet.

MICHAEL ACTON SMITH

Life is short; it's not a dress rehearsal. It's about grabbing it by the scruff of the neck and experiencing as many things and meeting as many people as possible. It's definitely not about sitting on the sofa and watching TV and moaning about what might have been.

LIZ MURRAY

We buried my mother the day after Christmas. I was sixteen years old. We had no money for a real funeral, so she was in a pine box with the lid nailed on. They wrote the words "head" and "feet" on this box. It was the most awful thing. We had a troubled life, but we had a very loving relationship, and my mother used to sit at the foot of my bed and share her dreams with me. About being sober, about getting a house, about having a better life. And at the end of all of her talks was that she was going to get around to doing it, but not right now. She would do it later; she would do it later. And I realized at some point that I was living my life telling myself I would do things later.

You might think, "I've got time to follow my dreams." You don't have time. Life is short. The current life expectancy is 24,869 days. While some of us will live more days and some fewer, either way you have only a precious number of days to live this life, and so you do not have time to put off your dreams. It is now or never. If you don't do it now, you will keep putting it off, and you'll never do it. The time is *now!*

"'Someday' is a disease that will take your dreams to the
grave with you..."

Timothy Ferriss

Author of The 4-Hour Workweek

Simply realizing that no one else is going to make your dreams
come true is a big step. Your boss, friends, partner, family, and
children cannot live your life for you. You are responsible for
creating a life that makes you happy and fulfilled. No one else
can do that for you.

MICHAEL ACTON SMITH

The most important thing people need to do is take
responsibility for their actions. It's very easy to blame
your upbringing or lack of money or lack of this or that.
But if you stop and say, "You know what? There is no one
ultimately responsible for my life but myself," that is the
really important step you can take to realize that you have to
shape things up. You have to change your mind-set. You have
to change that job. You have to change whatever it is to make
things happen.

LIZ MURRAY

When we're kids we're onto something that adults lose.
Everything is new and exciting, but also anything's really
possible. Then something happens. We fail, we get rejected,
we get disappointed. We atrophy that part of ourselves, and

we get way too serious. But what if you woke up every day and you just said, "What if I went for the things that I want? My dreams?" You hit the alarm clock, you put your feet on the floor, and you just go for it. To have that magic back in your life… to live for the sake of possibility.

You might be afraid to go after what you want in life because you think you could fail, but remember that you will never receive the call to follow a dream unless you have the wherewithal to accomplish that dream and turn it into a reality.

LAIRD HAMILTON
The fear of failure stops people from doing a lot of things. My mom used to have a saying, that we're each our greatest inhibitors – that we stop ourselves.

Another way we can stop ourselves is to think that there are no good ideas or opportunities left, and use that as our excuse not to make anything of our life. If you think there are no good opportunities, look at how easily Paul Orfalea found a golden opportunity.

While standing in a line to use a library photocopier, Paul Orfalea saw something that nobody else saw. He thought to himself, "If there's a line here, there must be lines in other places." And from that simple observation, the idea of Kinko's was born.

PAUL ORFALEA

If I have any good attributes, I know how to be in the present. You can't see opportunity if you are not in the moment.

MICHAEL ACTON SMITH

A lot of people look at successful people and just shrug it off and say, "Oh, they've been lucky." But in life you make your own luck, and when those opportunities come you are ready to jump on them.

ANASTASIA SOARE

Opportunities are in front of everybody every day. It's almost like a train station; everybody is in the station, there are trains that stop in front of people, but they have their eyes closed. They don't have their eyes open to see and get onto that train. Opportunities are everywhere.

G. M. RAO

You do not need a big dream to do a big thing. Just be open to life's opportunities.

"People will try to tell you that all of the great opportunities have been snapped up. In reality, the world changes every second, blowing new opportunities in all directions, including yours."

Ken Hakuta ~ Dr. Fad

Inventor

The Illusion of Security

Don't let money and security dictate your choices in life. Life continually changes; companies change hands, go bankrupt, or relocate overseas, jobs are lost, or economic collapse brings about massive cutbacks. You can lose your job, your savings, and your house. Marriages can end, health challenges can appear, and circumstances can arise that throw the security you thought you had out the door. I chose financial security over following my dreams, and when I was fired, I was clearly shown that the security I thought I had was all in my mind. Real security means knowing there *is* no security, because then you will make sure you live every day of your life to the fullest.

MASTIN KIPP

Family and friends, while they love you and while they want what's best for you, unless you have a kick-ass mom or dad or a kick-ass environment that you grew up in, generally they're going to want you to take the financially safe path where there's certainty and safety.

MICHAEL ACTON SMITH

As painful as it might be in the short term to step away from the security and a job that is paying well, you've got decades of life to live. You might as well suffer a bit of short-term pain to find something you love, even at a lower salary. Because if you do a job you love, you will end up being successful in so many other ways.

G. M. RAO

Don't let less money let you compromise on what you love to do. What you excel in will definitely bring you that very prosperity and security you need. Maybe the start would be small, but as one achieves perfection in what you are doing, everything else will follow.

Being trapped by security can happen to anyone; there are many people making a lot of money whose work is a grind to them, and they're as unfulfilled and unhappy as those making a lot less money.

LAIRD HAMILTON

What is money for you? If it's the goal then it will be the ruler of you — it'll dictate your movements and it'll control you.

Material things are wonderful, and experiencing them is one of the great pleasures of living on earth, but through the conditioning of society we can be misled into thinking that the accruement of material things is the purpose of our life. If material things were the purpose of our life they would provide true happiness, fulfillment, and satisfaction, and we'd never need to buy another thing. The happiness we feel when we get those things wouldn't be fleeting, but would be everlasting.

If accruing material things were our purpose in life, we would be able to take them with us when we leave. You would walk outside to get the paper in the morning and see that old man Joe's house across the street disappeared because he took it with him. We can't take material things with us because they are not who we are; while they are part of the joy of living on earth, they are not the purpose of our life.

LAYNE BEACHLEY

It was tough, it was challenging, and I sacrificed a lot, but I made those sacrifices out of choice, because following my dream of becoming a world champion was way more important to me than earning money.

We all need food, shelter, and clothing, but the pursuit of material things for their sake alone robs us of the freedom to live a truly fulfilling life. Don't let the tail wag the dog by making security and the pursuit of material things the purpose of your life instead of following your dreams. The irony is that when you do choose to follow your dreams over security, you will have it all, material riches and a rich, fulfilling life.

In addition, you receive something that money can never buy; you will have the greatest feeling of accomplishment, fulfillment, and satisfaction. Of course you will always want to do more and continue to build on your dreams, but when you experience that feeling of absolute fulfillment from taking the Hero's Journey, you'll be in no doubt that it was what you were born to do. And all that you gain within from fulfilling your purpose is what you *do* take with you when you leave.

Don't get to the end of your life and regret all the things you didn't do. Your life is precious. If you sell yourself out you won't find the happiness you desperately seek, because true happiness comes from fulfilling your dreams. Imagine what it would be like to get to the end of your life with no regrets. Imagine reflecting back on everything you did, and you are filled with the greatest feeling of satisfaction.

LIZ MURRAY

You know that saying, "Don't die with your music still inside of you"? People have things they dream of when they lay their head on the pillow at night. And if you don't honor that voice, it doesn't go anywhere. It's an energy that lives inside of you. You can't negate that energy. It's part of the fiber of who you are as a person. So if you put your head down on the pillow at night and you are called to do something in this world and you ignore that, then that dream is still locked inside of you. To me that's the worst thing… to die with your music inside of you.

A friend of mine worked for many years in the administration area of television, and through changes in the company she worked for she was pushed out of her job. She knew what she wanted to do more than anything, which was to be a movie director, and she started to make plans for a new life of living her dream. But just before she had seized the opportunity and put her new life into action as a movie director, she was offered a well-paying job back in television administration. She took the job, and just like that her dreams and the possibility of her new life vanished.

Michael Acton Smith

I don't want to get to the end of my life and be sitting in a nursing home and look back and wish I could have done all these things differently.

Anastasia Soare

What do you have to lose? You have to try it. You'll then live a life without knowing that you were able to do it. That's painful… to me, that's painful.

Paul Orfalea

I always tell students to start your business out of college. What's the worst thing that can happen to you? You can go live with your parents. It is not about experience – just stick your neck out and start your business.

Mastin Kipp

Most people won't take the leap, because they're not experiencing enough pain. Usually they will take action once they're so fed up, once they're so sick and tired, that they're like, "I can't take this anymore."

PAUL ORFALEA

Even if you're stuck in a job or a profession you don't like, you've got a better shot than ever in human history to end up doing something that really satisfies you.

Don't wait until you get to the point where you can't take it anymore before you make a change. Change your life now! Anything but true happiness and fulfillment is not good enough for you, so don't settle for anything less. Even if you think the tentacles of security have already wrapped themselves around you and you can't move because of your obligations, it's never too late – there are always unlimited ways to follow your dreams, and it is much easier than you think.

FINDING YOUR DREAM

Finding Your Dream

PETER FOYO

The absolute frustration of humankind – what do I do with my life?

LAYNE BEACHLEY

What do you want? Put your hand on your heart and ask yourself, what do I want? The first thing that comes to mind is always the right one.

Try and let go of the opinions, beliefs, and conclusions you have about yourself, because they're the very things that have prevented you from seeing your dream. Don't compare yourself with anyone else, because you have potential inside you that no one else on the planet has. Let go of all the limiting thoughts of what you think is possible for you, and open your mind to all possibilities. If you could let go of all the baggage you've accumulated in your life and wake up in the morning as though brand new, with a clean slate, every incredible possibility would be free to pour into your life!

LAYNE BEACHLEY
People look outside of themselves, but you know once you look inside yourself.

JOHN PAUL DEJORIA
We don't always know what we want, but we sure know what we don't want. Stop doing or thinking about what you don't want, and move on. It's like, if the train ride's a bad one, get off. You'll never experience anything else if you don't get off that train. Then you leave yourself open to something else.

MASTIN KIPP
Look at those moments where you're feeling blissful, moments when time just flies by, when you really feel lit up, when you really feel inspired. Think about, "Where have I been most inspired? Where have I really been happy?" Even if it was a few moments in your life, those are doorways showing you what your dream is about.

G. M. RAO
Some people will hit upon their big dream the moment they start thinking about their future.

What would you do if you could do anything? What would you do if money weren't a consideration at all? What would you do if success were guaranteed? When you ask any question, or you ask a question about your purpose, the Universe will transmit the answer to you. The answer doesn't come from your conscious mind; otherwise you would already know it. The answer comes from the Universal Mind.

LAYNE BEACHLEY

Most of us go through life not knowing what our dream is or what our purpose is, because we've never made the time to ask ourselves. It's important people take the time to identify what they love. If you don't, you're just a rudderless boat.

Before you ask any question, get yourself relaxed and in a calm state of mind. Then simply ask a question, like, "What is my purpose in life?" Or, "What am I meant to do?" Or, "What is my reason for being here?" Don't try and answer the question with your mind, but leave the question hanging in the air. Remain quiet for a minute, pay attention to anything that comes to you, and then take particular notice of what you're inspired to do during the day.

The answer will come into your mind in a flash, most likely when you're focused on something else altogether. Don't second-guess the answer when you get it, but think of one small step you can take toward it.

LAIRD HAMILTON

It's about listening to yourself, going inside, and being still. Go into the forest or go into the sea; be in a place where you can hear it. You'll be told by your own subconscious. You have it in you, and it's always been there, you've just put it someplace deep inside.

JOHN PAUL DeJORIA

Eventually if you open yourself up to the Universe it'll come to you.

A woman called Sara Blakely knew that she wanted to have a multimillion-dollar business, and that's all she knew. So Sara *asked* for a multimillion-dollar idea. One day while encountering a problem with her clothes when she was getting dressed, Sara got a brilliant idea for a new kind of women's underwear, and that idea became Spanx – now a multibillion-dollar global company.

PETER BURWASH

The other way is, go in the direction of the real entrepreneur, which is asking: "What does the world need and what does the world want at this particular point in time?"

MASTIN KIPP

"How could I solve a problem or some issue that people have?" Asking that question and figuring out whether that lines up with what you're passionate about is the key to

success. That's the sweet spot spiritually, emotionally, and also financially.

PAUL ORFALEA
Kinko's started with a question. If you've stopped asking questions, start asking them again.

Like Paul Orfalea, who created Kinko's, and Sara Blakely, who created Spanx, entrepreneurs ask questions. It's how entrepreneurs get a perfect idea at the perfect time, and it's exactly what the world needs. By simply asking a question they receive an idea, and from that idea they go on to create hugely successful companies.

Any time you need to ask any question, ask for information you need, ask for ideas, solutions, or the way to go with decisions, the answer will be transmitted to you from the Universal Mind, and appear in your mind as a flash. Make use of your ability to tap into this incredible resource!

PETER BURWASH
One way of finding out a direction: take two pieces of paper. Write down on one piece of paper what you're good at, and on the other piece of paper what you'd like to be able to do with your life. And see if you can take those two pages and match things together.

Mastin Kipp

Find people who have been on that journey, or ask people who are coming back from the road that you want to go down. Ask, "How did you do it?" Put yourself in an environment where people are doing the thing you want to do. Consume massive amounts of inspiring information, whether it's books or DVDs or CDs, because when you do that you're thinking the thoughts of the greatest people in the world.

Layne Beachley

You have to be clear. Clarity is what gives you power. Take the time to get clear on what you want and then you'll start taking a step toward it. But if you don't know what you want then you'll allow life to dictate the terms to you. I've never allowed life to dictate terms to me.

John Paul DeJoria

If you are dreaming about something and nothing's happening, write out what you want to achieve and have it in front of you when you wake up in the morning. One way or another, if you're focused on it, the mind leads you in that direction. Whatever the mind can conceive and believe it will achieve. The more you have something on your mind, the more it is going to happen.

Pete Carroll

It's not rocket science. To me it's really obvious that it's making a conscious decision about what you want to achieve

or what you want to become. It's the vision that sets in
motion whatever the powers are in the Universe that helps us
create what we want.

Even if you don't know yet what your dream is, there's
something you can do right now that will accelerate your dream
materializing: give your best to whatever you're currently doing.
Even if you know you ultimately want a different job than the one
you have, give your full attention to your current job, and give
your best to it. By doing this you will actually become bigger than
your current job, and in time doors will open to lead you to the
perfect fit of your dream!

LAIRD HAMILTON

A value that my mother instilled in me was, when you do
something, no matter what it is, do it to the best of your
ability. If you're a street sweeper, sweep the best you can.

JOHN PAUL DEJORIA

Success to me is not how much money you have; it's how
well you do what it is you do. Whether you're a janitor
or whether you're a businessperson or whether you're an
aviator, it's what you do and how well you do it dictates how
successful you are.

Big Dreams and Little Dreams

ANASTASIA SOARE

There's nothing wrong with small dreams. Big dreams are for people who are consciously willing to risk everything they have in life. There are small dreams, there are big dreams, and there are crazy dreams. It takes a certain personality to go so crazy.

MICHAEL ACTON SMITH

Most people don't have big dreams in life. They don't have the confidence. They think all of the exciting stuff is done by other people. But having big dreams is important, and it does make life exciting. If you don't have big dreams, big dreams can't come true.

ANASTASIA SOARE

People need to understand how much they want to give to get. Everything in life is like a bank account. Whatever you put in, you will get out. Don't put little and expect to get big. It is not going to happen.

Someone might start out with a really big dream, while someone else might start out with a small dream that becomes far bigger than they could have imagined. Life seems to call us to a dream that is a size we can handle at the time.

G. M. RAO
Little dreams, like pieces in a puzzle, will open out the larger dream. Initially, to even dream is difficult, but it's important to know that Mahatma Gandhi never started off with any big dream. He just kept pushing the limits of what he wanted to happen, and bingo, the biggest thing happened.

When you find your dream and make it come true, all the other smaller dreams you have for your life come true too. One of my dreams in my twenties was to live in a different country. I wanted the adventure and challenge of living in a country that was unfamiliar to me, and experiencing the excitement of a different culture from the one I knew. When my dream of *The Secret* came true, my work required me to move from Australia to the United States, and so a dream I had put aside came true at the same time as my big dream. Dreams are attached to each other, and once one comes, all the rest will follow.

Whether you've found your dream or you have no idea what your dream is, there is one extremely simple piece of advice that if followed, will positively lead you to your dream.

FOLLOW YOUR BLISS

Follow Your Bliss

Joseph Campbell was one of the world's most well respected mythologists, and through his insightful teachings he gave us a simple yet profound message for our life:

"Follow Your Bliss."

These three words are the compass for your life; they tell you what direction to point toward in every moment. Bliss is how you feel when you do something you absolutely love to do, and it is a thread that's connected to your dreams. So when you follow your bliss you also find your dreams, and fulfill your reason for being here.

Nick Woodman knew he wanted to be an entrepreneur, but he didn't have a clue in what area of business. While he was following his bliss surfing with his friends on a trip to Australia and Indonesia, Nick kept thinking how great it would be to have a camera that could capture the action of him and his friends surfing. That one little thought was the seed of an idea that became the GoPro camera, which made Nick Woodman one of the world's youngest billionaire entrepreneurs.

Bliss Leads to Bliss

There's an irresistible and powerful quality that radiates from you when you're in bliss and doing what you love, and that powerful quality draws more bliss to you. Even though you might not be able to see your dream yet, when you're in bliss you are on the very path that will lead you to it.

LAYNE BEACHLEY

Make the choice to do something that makes you feel good on a daily basis. How many people do that? How many people identify what makes them feel good and then commit that time to themselves on a daily basis?

You are following your bliss when you make a decision to do something that makes you feel really good every day. It could be as simple as sitting in a park or a garden and relaxing with your feet up, or buying a cup of your favorite coffee and instead of drinking it on the run, sitting down, taking a breath, and just watching the world pass by. No matter how insignificant or small it might seem, each day make sure to do something that is your idea of bliss. Before you know it, you will be inspired with other blissful things you can do, and, from just doing that one thing, you will soon have a hold of a thread that's going to take you to your dreams and to a far better life.

PETER FOYO

It's a cliché, but I believe it's really important to live your life to the absolute fullest.

MICHAEL ACTON SMITH

Along with our family and our relationships, the job we do is one of the most important parts of our life. It's certainly somewhere you spend most of your waking hours, so it should be something enjoyable; it should be something that you are passionate about and that you care about.

JOHN PAUL DEJORIA

I love what I do, or I wouldn't be doing it.

G. M. RAO

Money and security are very important to everyone. Personal satisfaction and passion for a particular thing you do is more important. That is why it is important to dream.

If you have a full-time job, you probably spend around 250 days of the year at work. Two hundred and fifty days is over two-thirds of the year, so if you're not doing what sets your heart on fire and fills you with passion and excitement, you are wasting a lot of precious days of your life.

> "Your work is going to fill a large part of your life, and the only way to be truly satisfied is to do what you believe is great work. And the only way to do great work is to love what you do. If you haven't found it yet, keep looking and don't settle."

Steve Jobs

Cofounder of Apple Inc.

If you're at home raising children, make sure this precious time of your life includes something that you love, and do it as often as you can. When I was at home raising my children I needed a creative outlet, and so I threw myself into cooking. I took cooking courses, bought books, and practiced and cooked until I had perfected every cooking method I could find. Cooking became my bliss. When I returned to my job in television, the first television show I developed was a cooking show, and because of what I had learned, the show became very successful. With its success, my career in television production flourished.

JOHN PAUL DEJORIA
When you are passionate and you like what you're doing, when it is what you want to do, not what you have to do, you always do it better because you're doing it with love.

For some reason many of us have separated our bliss from our work, and we don't love what we do every day. But life doesn't have to be like that. The fact that there are people who are blissful and living their dream for their work tells you that it's possible for you, too. You don't need to know what your dream job is, because your bliss is connected to it, so all you have to do is follow your bliss and it will lead you to it!

G. M. RAO

I don't work because I have to work. I work because I enjoy the work. To me work is worship, because it is with a sense of purpose and gives happiness and contentment not just to me but to those around me.

LIZ MURRAY

I don't think I've ever said: "I'm going to work."

What kind of job can you imagine yourself doing where you wouldn't ever say, "I'm going to work"? Your work should embrace your passion or special talent, and be something you would do whether you were paid or not.

LIZ MURRAY

I have to have fun in what I do. If I don't have some kind of fun, if it doesn't blow my hair back, if it doesn't feel like magic, I just can't stick with that. I must pursue things that make me feel like it's Christmas morning when I was a kid and I couldn't wait to get out of bed. If I start dreading

something or wanting it to end, it's a symptom that
something needs to change.

MICHAEL ACTON SMITH
At Mind Candy we love working with people who don't take
themselves too seriously, who can have fun as they work.
None of this is life or death, even though some people would
like to think of it like that. I think you enjoy life and you have
a lighter spirit when you have fun at work.

"I didn't set out to be rich. The fun and the challenge
in life were what I wanted – and still do… but I have
found that, if I have fun, the money will come."

Sir Richard Branson

Entrepreneur/Business Magnate

Be True to Yourself

When your work is your bliss, you will be happy. Doing a job
you think you should do instead of doing what you love is
leading a false life. So many precious people are living a life that
has been put upon them by well-meaning parents, teachers, or
society, or even by a friend or partner, and they're miserable.
We're seeing the evidence of the misery in people through the
alarming increase of mental health problems in the world. Shut

out what everyone else thinks, have the courage to follow your own bliss, and you will be immensely happy.

John Paul DeJoria

There's a lot of things one wants to do that maybe isn't commonplace or that everyone else agrees with, but if it makes you happy, by gosh, go after it. It's so rewarding, being true to yourself.

Michael Acton Smith

I left university and got a sensible job in a bank, and I realized quite quickly that it just wasn't for me. It didn't speak to my soul. And I realized I was pretty much unemployable.

G. M. Rao

When we pursue a dream, there will be several pulls from different directions, from stakeholders, family, friends, and society. In my case, there were many such situations. For example, when my brothers with whom I was in partnership for our family business had different aspirations, I exited the partnership to pursue my own dreams.

G. M. Rao had the courage to follow his own dreams, and look what he's done with his life. He has built airports, highways, and hospitals, and developed cities in India. He has improved his country and the lives of hundreds of millions of people because he made a decision to follow his own bliss.

It often takes courage to do the thing you love and go against the majority. Resist the temptation to try and please anyone, and be true to yourself. It's not your job to please anybody else, anyway; it's their job to please themselves and find their own happiness. This is your life, and you must follow your own heart. There is something special about you, a talent or skill that is unique to you, and you have a responsibility to your life to bring it out.

> "Take a job that you love. I think you are out of your
> mind if you keep taking jobs that you don't like
> because you think it will look good on your resume.
> Isn't that a little like saving up sex for your old age?"

Warren Buffett

Business Magnate and Investor

ANASTASIA SOARE

Look into your life. If you are happy where you are, good for you. If you are not happy, you should start analyzing. "Okay, what makes me happy? I'm in a job and I'm unhappy." Well, change the job.

If you've decided that you're going to make a change but you don't know how, the first and biggest step you can take is to start to follow your bliss.

ANASTASIA SOARE

You are an accountant, and you are totally unhappy. Well, maybe you like to cook. Go and become a chef. Don't drop your job immediately, because you need to pay your bills, but try to set the plan. "Okay, I'm going to do this part time." You have to plan. Every penny that I made I wanted to make sure I would use to follow my dream. If you do not have that support from money, the stress that comes from not being able to pay your bills will shatter your dream.

Anastasia had a family to support, and so she spent two years planning her business before she took the leap. Now she has a global company and she's living the life of her dreams. If Anastasia hadn't worked on a plan and followed her bliss, she would still be working fourteen-hour days in someone else's salon.

There are so many things you can start doing now to follow your bliss. Take a free course on what you would love to do. Get books and magazines and read up on the people who are doing what you want to do. Find out what kind of job you could get to put you into that field. Use the Internet, social media, write blogs, and do research. You have the world at your fingertips and more opportunities than ever to connect and explore. Put as much attention as you can into what you would love to do.

LAIRD HAMILTON

How do you transition from what you're doing into a place where you're doing what you love? Subsidize doing what you love to do with doing something else in order to give you enough support to do the thing you love. All of a sudden you will be doing the thing you love as the thing that provides for you. And that transition will occur much quicker than you think.

MASTIN KIPP

If you have other responsibilities you can slowly start to build up a side business, and eventually you just take the leap.

"Follow your bliss and the Universe will open doors for you where there were only walls."

Joseph Campbell
                    Mythologist

You can begin right now to follow your bliss, because somewhere in your life there is something you've always wanted to do that you haven't done yet. Have you had an urge to learn ballroom dancing or rap, surfing, or white water rafting? Have you had an urge to take an acting class, a painting or gardening class, or to learn how to style clothes or the interior of houses? Or is there a musical instrument that you've had the urge to learn because when you hear it played you immediately go into a state of bliss?

Do you feel drawn to a particular country, and when you hear the language being spoken something inside you stirs? Was there something you loved doing as a child, but as you grew into adulthood you put it aside because you had to make a living? What is it that you've always wanted to do?

Most people either never get around to acting on these urges or they put them aside because they think they're insignificant and have no relationship to the bigger things they want in their life. But that urge you feel to do something in particular is the Universe calling you to follow your bliss, and that particular thing is definitely connected to the path of your dreams. You can't see the connection from your perspective on earth, but the Universe can clearly see it's the path that will lead you to your dreams.

The Thing that Moves You

What are you drawn to? What moves you? What have you always had the desire to do? Follow that urge; follow your bliss, because while you might not consider it relevant to your dream, it is in fact the very thread that will lead you there – as it did for my daughter.

From the moment she learned to read, my daughter said she was going to be an author when she grew up. Aside from writing, she loved two things more than anything else: being in nature and horse riding. She maintained her love of all three from childhood into adulthood, but when she moved to America she had to leave her horses behind.

With her relocation, her lifelong dream of becoming an author sat quietly in the background, while another big dream took over her – to meet her perfect partner and have a family. She made a list of everything she wanted in her perfect partner, but for some months he was nowhere to be seen.

Then she made a decision to just follow her bliss. So she started horse-riding lessons, she started to write again, and she bought a little house surrounded by nature. Her little house needed a *lot* of work, but she was blissfully happy living in it, because she was surrounded by nature.

Here's what happened when my daughter followed her bliss. She was given a new horse to ride in her lesson, and the moment she got on that horse they were at one with each other. She had found the horse of her dreams, and she was given the opportunity to buy the horse in gradual payments she could easily manage. She came up with an idea for a children's book, and she finished writing her first book. She was blissfully happy; she had her dream horse, she was living in nature, and she'd finally written a book.

And right there and then, amid her bliss, my daughter met her perfect partner. Two months after the dream of her perfect partner came true, her lifelong dream of becoming an author also came true; a major publisher accepted her book for publication! On top of that, things were suddenly looking promising for her little house in need of a lot of work – her perfect partner just happens to be the son of a builder!

You can have it all. No matter how unrelated you think your bliss might be to a bigger dream, follow your bliss and follow it with all of your heart. Although you can't see the whole way ahead, your bliss is the thread that will lead you to *all* of your dreams!

Part Two
The Hero

BELIEF

Belief

LAYNE BEACHLEY

Ultimately, to achieve anything in life you have to believe that you can. That belief is what allowed me to win many world titles.

LAIRD HAMILTON

You need to believe that all things are possible – that you can do it.

To believe in yourself is perhaps the most powerful hero ability you have available to you. Your belief will carry you through every difficult situation or any challenging circumstances, and enable you to ultimately realize your dream!

In his first season as head coach at the University of Southern California, Pete Carroll mentored a talented young quarterback whose great potential threatened to go unfulfilled. The problem was that this player was prone to negative self-talk, which at times affected his ability to perform. Once Pete discovered his quarterback anticipated making mistakes, he worked with his staff to eliminate the player's negative self-talk.

Thanks to their timely intervention, the quarterback came to believe in himself, so much so that two seasons later he was awarded the Heisman Trophy as the best player in all college football. He went on to star in the NFL, and won "Most Valuable Player" in the NFL Pro Bowl. His name is Carson Palmer.

PETE CARROLL

Throughout my coaching life, I've helped people understand the power of their thoughts and personal beliefs. A person's self-talk is the clearest indicator of one's belief in themselves. I constantly preach the value and significance of positive self-talk as a key element to manifesting your dreams.

ANASTASIA SOARE

The message I want to send to people is: if I came here without speaking the language, with not one penny in my pocket, and I was able to do this, anybody could do it. You need just to believe in yourself. That's it.

But what if you don't believe in yourself?

The only reason you don't believe in yourself is because you've inadvertently *thought* your way into not believing in yourself. Thinking a whole bunch of thoughts and accepting that they're true forms beliefs. You were born with belief in yourself, and so if you don't believe in yourself today it just means that in your life you have accepted thoughts about yourself that other people put upon you, and you believed them to be true. And the only way you have maintained that lack of belief has been through your own continuing thoughts about yourself – your self-talk.

MASTIN KIPP

The number-one hindrance to success is people who believe it's not possible for them. If you believe something's not possible, then you're right. And the whole Universe will be against you, not because the Universe is a bad place, but because that's how you're interacting with it, and all you'll look for is proof of your low self-worth, and proof of why it's not possible.

The way to change a lack of belief is very simple. Begin thinking the opposite thoughts to what you've been thinking about yourself: that you *can* do it, and that you have everything within you to do it. Remind yourself that you have incredibly powerful abilities, and that you will know exactly how to use them when the time comes. Remind yourself that all you need to do is take one step at a time.

Your Subconscious Mind

As you think thoughts that you can achieve your dream, you will change the program in your subconscious mind. Your subconscious mind is like a computer, and it has many different programs that you have loaded into it, either with your thoughts or by listening to and accepting other people's thoughts about you. And you've been doing this throughout your life.

MICHAEL ACTON SMITH
If you don't believe in yourself – if you don't believe you can achieve something – then no one else is going to.

All the programs in your subconscious mind have been put there by thought, and it's thought and thought alone that will create a new program and override the old one.

When you first start to think thoughts that you can do anything, you'll feel the rejection from the "firewall" of your subconscious mind, which will tell you that those thoughts aren't true. But as you keep planting the thought that you can do it, eventually those thoughts will become a belief, and you will have changed the program.

LAYNE BEACHLEY
Anyone can acquire self-belief if they choose to do so.

It's surprising that after many years – even a lifetime – of not believing in yourself, it only takes a short time of concerted effort to start believing in yourself.

The most powerful time to reprogram the subconscious mind is when you're falling asleep at night. When you're in that very sleepy state of being half asleep and half awake, plant the thought that you can do anything and you can achieve anything you set your mind to. Your aim is to make that "believing in yourself" thought your last thought before you fall asleep, because the very last thought you think as you're falling asleep goes straight past the firewall and into your subconscious mind. And when that thought goes past the firewall, the subconscious mind must accept it as true.

Once your subconscious mind has the new program of believing, it must carry out that program and prove your belief in yourself true. You will suddenly find new people in your life who believe in you, or new support from people already in your life, and you will feel inspired to take particular steps or actions that prove your own abilities and increase your self-belief.

Whatever you hold in your subconscious mind is what happens in your life. This is because any new program in your subconscious mind is immediately transmitted to the Universal Mind; and once the Universe has the instructions, it will work with you to make sure you achieve what you believe. Perhaps now you will understand why it has been said that "whatever the mind of man can conceive and *believe* he can achieve."

G. M. RAO

I strongly believed in my vision of creating value for society. In spite of two significant setbacks that could have derailed my life, I persevered because my values and unflinching commitment were aligned with the will of the Universe, which supported me unconditionally. There was never a doubt in my mind.

LAIRD HAMILTON

I truly believed I could achieve my dream. I couldn't have achieved what I've been able to do without truly believing it. Now, it doesn't mean I didn't have doubt, because doubt is ever-present, always looming and circling and trying to get a hold of you. But I didn't embrace the doubt.

Believing in yourself doesn't mean there won't be moments where you question your ability to achieve your dream. In those moments of doubt, just bring your mind back to the very next step you have to take, because you'll find it's easier to believe you can take the next tiny step rather than have your head spinning with the whole journey ahead. And when you think about it, you can only take one step at a time on the Hero's Journey, and one step at a time is all that every successful person took.

When you're feeling happy, your belief will be strong. If you're feeling tired, discouraged, under the weather, or lacking energy, that's when doubts come in. Everyone has those moments, so remind yourself that the way you're feeling is temporary, and it *will* pass. That's why it's so important to follow your bliss every day, because in doing that you will be happy, and as a consequence, your belief will be strong.

G. M. RAO

You have to invest belief in your dream; be confident that what you want is simply the best thing in the world for you. Without that belief, what follows is a halfhearted approach without effort, determination, or persistence. Many times, the fear of failure is behind this lack of conviction.

MASTIN KIPP

My mom told me I can do anything I set my mind to. So I literally believed her. I knew from the beginning that when I really set my mind to something, something big will happen.

LAIRD HAMILTON

My mother believed that I could walk on water. Her belief was less about the goal and more that I could be a good person, but that gave me the strength to believe in myself. Everybody who's got somebody who believes in them has got to hold on to that person. That's the person they need to be around.

ANASTASIA SOARE

A little thing will change your life. These were more innocent times, but I vividly remember when I was six years old in my mother and father's tailor shop, one day my mother said: "You remember every time I take you to the shop? I will write on a piece of paper what to buy and give you the money. You take the bus, and count six stops. Make sure you ask the driver if it's the right stop." I said, "Mom, I'm six years old! I don't know…" "No, you are smart. You can do it." I was a little afraid, but you know what was in my mind? She said that I am smart and I could do it, and if she said that then I am smart. I came back, and I will never forget the smile on her face. She said, "I told you you're smart and you could do it. I'm so proud of you."

MICHAEL ACTON SMITH
Self-belief is easier when you start with supportive parents, but it's definitely not impossible to do it without them.

Even if you didn't have a parent who helped you instill belief in yourself, there was someone in your childhood who believed in you. It could have been a relative, grandparent, neighbor, teacher, or sibling, but there was definitely at least one person who believed in you when you were growing up. And whether that person is still alive or not, you literally have all the support in the world available to you now.

When you decide to follow your dream, the Universe will support you and provide you with every circumstance, every person, and everything else you need to make your dream come true. And the way to leverage the Universe is to use your subconscious mind to believe!

LAIRD HAMILTON

Believe things will take care of themselves if you just focus on your mission or your goals, and that you will be provided for because of the effort you put forth.

MASTIN KIPP

Make a list of who inspires you, and then write out what about that person inspires you. Is it their tenacity? Is it how much they give? Is it their bank account? Is it their brand? Is it what they've done to the world? Then recognize that the thing that inspires you about that person is actually a part of yourself.

LIZ MURRAY

We learn by doing, and so if you can place yourself in situations, through experiential learning you can rebuild self-esteem and you can shift your belief system. You can do things that previously didn't seem possible because you had no example of it in your life. It's almost like a muscle memory. So new experiences can bring us to new belief.

Your belief will increase and strengthen with every step you take and every experience you have on the Hero's Journey, as you discover for yourself what you are truly capable of.

Believe in your dream and believe in you, because you are a hero, and the hero within you doesn't just believe you can achieve your dream – it *knows* you will!

Vision

MASTIN KIPP
The Bible says it best: without a vision, people perish.

LAIRD HAMILTON
Every idea that I've ever had and everything I've ever done I first saw it in my mind. People talk about visualization; that's just a way of saying that you can see it in your mind. Ultimately you can't have a dream without being able to see it. How are you going to manifest something that you don't see in your mind first?

Sports people and athletes know the power of creating a vision of their dream. You will have heard one athlete after another at the Olympic Games talk about the fact that they had played this moment of winning gold in their mind for four years. Athletes use the technique of visualizing constantly in their training to see everything they want to achieve in their mind, and to practice and improve specific skills.

LAYNE BEACHLEY

I spent a lot of time visualizing as an athlete. The great thing about being an athlete is utilizing that technique to visualize the desired outcome.

PETE CARROLL

Constantly we work with visualization, with envisioning what we could become. All power comes from the ability to envision what you want to become. How could you possibly get there unless you can picture it? You wouldn't know when you had arrived.

"When I'm about to fall asleep, I visualize to the point that I know exactly what I want to do: dive, glide, stroke, flip, reach the wall, hit the split time to the hundredth, then swim back again for as many times as I need to finish the race."

Michael Phelps

Olympic Champion Swimmer

The sporting world has latched on to one of the most powerful practices to create what we want – create a vision in our mind of the exact outcome we want. Despite all the success that's achieved in sports by using this technique, people generally are still unaware of the fact that they can use this same technique to create success in their life.

LAYNE BEACHLEY

I could only visualize one outcome, and that was standing on the podium with the trophy above my head, being sprayed with champagne. That's all that mattered to me.

The most important part of creating a vision is that you get a picture in your mind of the end result or the outcome you want. Get every other detail out of your mind of how you're going to achieve it, and just see the end result of your dream. Layne Beachley chose the vision of standing on the winning podium being sprayed with champagne because that vision clearly represented the outcome she wanted – becoming a world champion.

MICHAEL ACTON SMITH

I love drawing and doodling and sketching, and I spend hours filling up notebooks. I scribble down the things that I want to achieve and do.

When you sketch elements of your dream, your mind immediately forms a vision from your sketch. When you write notes about your dream, your mind automatically forms a vision from your notes. Either way, you're visualizing.

In my life, whenever I have to do something I've never done before, I never think of going into it without first having visualized the outcome I want. I play that vision over in my mind, and feel the excited feelings as though it has already happened. I don't think about how I will do it, I just visualize the outcome I want. This technique is one of the most powerful and little known abilities that human beings have to create whatever they want in their life. Because your subconscious mind loves pictures, when you have placed a picture in your subconscious mind it must do everything to make it materialize.

G. M. RAO

My dream was always in my mind. Right from the beginning I was living with my dream alive in me, acting it out even when it was just tendrils of thought. My actions arose from the thought that my dream had already happened, and from my actions I could see the results arise.

"Success is achieved twice. Once in the mind and the second time in the real world."

Azim Premji
Indian Business Tycoon

PETER FOYO

Virtually everything I've done in my life is not as a result of what I've studied or of how hard I worked. It's a result of visualizing and knowing I'm already there.

When I was making *The Secret* film, I visualized the outcome I wanted multiple times during a day. I saw the outcome so clearly in my mind that it felt as though it had already happened. There's no doubt in my mind that visualization was the most powerful thing I did to help make *The Secret* a huge success.

PETER FOYO

People think you're an outright liar when you're visualizing, because they think, "That's not happening. That's not here." Oh, yes it is. Absolutely it's here, because if you can think it, it can happen.

Once you have got good at visualizing the outcome of your dream in your mind, where you feel as though it has already happened, you can use the same technique for any smaller steps or goals you want to achieve on the Hero's Journey. But even if you only ever visualize the end result of what you want, your vision ensures that you will get there, somehow, some way.

LIZ MURRAY

Because my goal was straight A's, I went to the office in my school and I asked them to print out my transcripts. They said, "You just started. You don't have any." I said, "No, I want the blank ones." They printed it out with my name on it, and I sat in the staircase and wrote my grades in. I felt like they already existed in the future, I just had to catch up with it. When I did homework I would take out the straight A's I decided I would have and put them on the side so I could look at them while I was working. I really worked from a feeling that it was already real somewhere.

In your life, you can use visualization for any situation you want to go well. You can visualize the outcome of exams, auditions, interviews, meetings, pitches, proposals, making a speech, meeting your in-laws, taking a trip, or your boss giving you the biggest raise in the history of your company!

Make sure you visualize where you want to be at the end of this year, and maintain a yearly vision with every New Year. In addition, create a bigger vision of where you want to be five years from now. Just watch what happens with your life!

> "You've got to visualize where you're headed and be very clear about it. Take a Polaroid picture of where you're going to be in a few years."
>
> *Sara Blakely*
> Founder of Spanx

JOHN PAUL DEJORIA

I wake up in the morning and I just am. In other words, I don't turn on the TV, I don't get my cup of coffee. I don't do anything. I just sit there in bed, and I just am. There are no decisions to make, no phone calls to make. Just for five minutes, I try and clear my mind and I am in the here and now. This way your mind goes forth during the day uncluttered. And if you have a dream you're trying to achieve, in the last couple of minutes you think a little bit about that and how much you want it, why you want it, and things you can do to help get closer to it.

When you stop the franticness of the day before it starts, and you get your mind into a state of complete relaxation, the vision of your dream will slide straight into your subconscious mind. It's much like shutting down your computer to install a new update or program. Updates can't be installed while your computer is running lots of other programs – and likewise your subconscious mind can't receive your vision if your mind is on the run with other things. But when you shut down your mind through relaxation, your vision will be successfully installed.

When you use visualization successfully, the people around you will wonder how it can be that all of a sudden everything is going your way, and everything works out for you as though you're some kind of superhuman. And you will know that you're just using one of the simplest, but most powerful abilities you were born with, and which is available to every human being on the planet.

THE MIND OF A HERO

The Mind of a Hero

PETER BURWASH

You wake up in the morning and you've really only got one major decision; it's not about the clothes you're going to wear, it's not about how you're going to do your hair. It's, are you going to have a good attitude or are you going to have a bad attitude? Because a positive attitude is so critical.

MICHAEL ACTON SMITH

I am very lucky to naturally be an optimistic person, and I think that helped enormously.

One of the most difficult things every human being wrestles with is their attitude. When you really get it that you'll thwart your own success, be miserable, and potentially make yourself sick unless you adopt a positive attitude, you will choose to start looking at life through optimistic eyes. Your attitude is of your own creation. And it can be your biggest undoing or your most powerful tool.

LAYNE BEACHLEY

If you want things to improve in your life, if you want a change from the patterns that you're currently experiencing, then learn to take responsibility for your thoughts.

Your thoughts form your attitude, and so the first step in changing your attitude is to take responsibility for your own thoughts. When you can recognize and accept that it's the thoughts you are thinking that are making you feel miserable, then you will begin to change the kinds of thoughts you think.

If someone offered you the life of your dreams in exchange for you finding as many good things every day as you could, you would do it in a flash. Well, that is the way you receive the life of your dreams!

PETE CARROLL

In my life I have found that thinking positively and living in optimism is the best way to be successful and create the things you want.

If you look to outside circumstances in the world to form your attitude, you'll be in trouble. That would require every circumstance around you to be perfect all the time so you could have a positive attitude, and you cannot control every circumstance. It would also require a lot of people to behave perfectly all the time, and you cannot control anyone but yourself. If you think about it, you would actually need all 7 billion of us to shape up into what you want so you can have an optimistic and positive attitude. You simply can't look to outside circumstances to dictate what kind of attitude you will have. If you do, you will always find a circumstance or a person that will give you a reason to have a negative attitude. In order to become your most powerful tool, your attitude must be dictated from *within*.

MASTIN KIPP
I've been optimistic in the worst of circumstances.

PETER BURWASH
Everything has a positive or a negative to it. You can find both in every single situation in the world. The person who's going to succeed is the person who's going to be able to look at things in a positive manner first.

You have the freedom to choose to be optimistic or pessimistic. You can peel off your old attitude like a suit of clothes, and put on a brand spanking new attitude every single day. It's as simple as that.

Something Good is Just About to Happen

PETE CARROLL

My mom always said that something good is just about to happen. I didn't realize this early on, but I've lived my life with the thought that no matter how dark or how difficult things become, there's this consistent hope that it's just about to turn. My mom gave me the gift of that. It keeps me positive and keeps me always looking toward things in an optimistic manner. I've been very fortunate to live my life with that thought.

Because of the duality on earth, there are always going to be both positive and negative experiences. But if you consistently look for the good and maintain a positive attitude despite outside circumstances, you will triumph. And there are no better words to remember to help you maintain a positive attitude than Pete Carroll's mom's words: "Something good is just about to happen!" If you always know that something good is just about to happen, your optimism will never waiver for long.

G. M. RAO

My spirituality helped me think positively even when things looked bleak.

People who are happy and successful think more about the good things that can happen, think more about having happiness, having money, and creating a rich and meaningful life, than they do the opposite of those things.

G. M. RAO

I have encountered so many well-educated people from wealthy backgrounds and of a high social standing who are not able to succeed because of their negative attitudes. Negativity pulls one down.

A pessimistic attitude toward life means a miserable life. At some point in your life you've no doubt encountered someone who is pessimistic about everything, and when you are with him or her it sucks the energy and the joy out of you. Well, that's precisely what a pessimistic attitude does to you.

ANASTASIA SOARE

If you are a pessimist and you are depressed all the time that is going to kill any dream.

On the other hand, I'm sure you've known someone who is always up and has a cheerful and bright attitude toward life, and when you are with him or her you also feel fantastic and full of life. And that's what an optimistic attitude does to you.

Show me one pessimistic person who is deliriously happy in every part of their life. It's not possible, because even if they had everything they wanted, the glass would still look half empty to them!

PETER BURWASH

Two people are living side by side and one person wakes up in the morning and throws open the window and says; "Good morning, God!" And then the person next door, the pessimist, says; "Good God. It's morning."

Just ask yourself whether you think blaming and complaining can transform a person's life into success and happiness. Do you think whining and criticizing can fulfill a person's dreams and give them everlasting happiness?

PETE CARROLL

One of the rules that always applies in our program is no whining, no complaining, and no excuses. They're not the kind of thought patterns that support. That's not going to take us at all where we want to go.

Do you ever see Superman whining? Do you ever see Indiana Jones complaining? Do you see James Bond blaming others for his lot in life? You'll never see movie superheroes display any of these traits, because the moviemakers know that the superhero would immediately be diminished in your eyes and would no longer be a hero. And the audience would instinctively feel something was wrong; how can such a negative person become a hero? And the answer is, they can't.

Blame, resentment, whining, and complaining are excuses we make when we're not living the life we came here to live.

LIZ MURRAY

In our darker moments as human beings we start getting angry and entitled and blaming. I think anger, entitlement, and blame are all cousins of each other; they're about what you should have had and what you're lacking and who should have given it to you. I grew up thinking nobody owed me anything. Realize that anything you have you're blessed to have, because it could just as easily disappear. That's a much better attitude to have.

Because we see people around us who blame and resent and whine and complain, we can get the mistaken impression that it's okay and won't harm us. But all of those negative emotions will pull you down and down and disempower you until you feel hopeless. None of those emotions can ever fill you with the happiness you want and deserve. None of those emotions will lead you to your dream. None of them are befitting of the hero that you are.

LAIRD HAMILTON

It's impossible that you're going to be all cheery, happy, smiley, everything's perfect all the time. There's going to be jealousy, there's going to be envy; all those negative things are going to occur at times. That's just part of being a human. But do you give them ground to grow, or do you push them out and fill them with the positive things? What do you spend the majority of your time doing and thinking and saying? That's what's going to bear the fruit for you.

A positive and optimistic attitude doesn't mean you don't have occasional down days. You *will* have some down days. It's not about the occasional down days, though; it's about how many of the 24,869 precious days of your life you're enjoying because of your positive and optimistic attitude.

PETE CARROLL

Try to operate on a daily basis with a quieted mind, not a mind that's always second-guessing and wondering if you're worthy. Negative thoughts like, "I don't know if I can handle this," "This is too big for me," "I've never been here before," "In the past I've come up short here or there," draw your focus away from performing like you're capable. We are likely to carry those thoughts with us and we won't be as good as we could be.

LAYNE BEACHLEY

Be aware of how you're feeling, because there are times when you do feel negative, you feel down, or you feel defeated, and the most important thing you can do is accept responsibility, acknowledge that those feelings have emanated from the way you're thinking, and choose to do something different to alter your current circumstances.

If you're feeling down, then do something that makes you feel really good and lifts your spirits. Think about the best thing you can do right in this moment that will make you feel as good as you can feel, and do it.

LAYNE BEACHLEY

To make myself feel happy and positive, I first have to do something I love and build a sense of satisfaction within myself. So every day I go surfing, because I know that makes me feel very happy and satisfied.

The mind of a hero is a predominantly positive mind. The attitude of a hero is consistently optimistic. Together, a positive mind and an optimistic attitude are an incredibly powerful tool to realize your dreams, because your thoughts and your attitude become your life!

THE HEART OF A HERO

The Heart of a Hero

Courage

LAIRD HAMILTON
Fear is an ever-present emotion in us. It's part of what made us evolve.

LIZ MURRAY
You can never get rid of fear, because fear is a physiological response. You can hook someone up to a machine and you can see you're having a fear response. You're always going to have a fear response.

Although we are each an individual, we are all human, and so every one of us has the full gamut of human emotions, such as fear, uncertainty, doubt, joy, passion, hope, and belief. At different times on the Hero's Journey you will experience every one of these emotions. Just because someone is successful doesn't mean they didn't experience the same feelings of fear, uncertainty, and doubt. Fear is the same for them as it is for you. Doubt is the same for them as it is for you. The successful person just decided to continue following their dream despite feeling those emotions. They didn't allow their fear or doubt to paralyze them or stop them from achieving their dream.

MASTIN KIPP

Whether your dream is big or even if it's just a small dream, it's still outside your comfort zone, and stepping outside your comfort zone equates to fear. But fear is perhaps one of the most misunderstood entities in human development. From a biological perspective fear is designed to keep us safe; fear is self-preservation.

We experience two kinds of fear as humans. But it's important to understand that our physiological instinct that protects our survival is not the same as psychological fear.

Psychological fear is something we create with our own minds when there is no danger to our survival. You may have experienced this kind of fear if you've had to take a final exam that you felt your future depended on, or if you took a test for your driver's license. You may have felt psychological fear if you competed in a sporting event at your school, or if you had to stand up and make a speech in front of a lot of people. In all of these situations there was no threat to your life; the fear you felt was psychological, a fear created by your own mind. Most of us will only face psychological fear on the Hero's Journey, but some, such as an athlete performing an extreme sport, may experience both kinds of fear at the same time.

LAIRD HAMILTON

People say, "You're not scared." Actually, no. I think I'm the most scared. I'm scared of those big waves. But your imagination is always greater than the reality. Subjecting yourself to the thing you fear is probably the most important way of becoming acclimated to it, becoming intimate with it, and all of a sudden it doesn't have the power that it had.

In fantasy movies you see the hero face dragons or monsters that he or she has to slay to accomplish their quest. In movies, the hero's quest represents our life and what we have to go through in order to fulfill our dream. The monsters are the doubts and fears of our own mind, and just like in movies we have to overcome them and not let them prevent us from fulfilling our dream.

The very act of doing something that is out of your comfort zone slays the monsters and dragons of fear and doubt on the spot.

MASTIN KIPP

If you want to live a fearless life, never leave your comfort zone, ever, ever. If you want to grow – and ultimately what's going to make you happy is growth – you will be required to constantly step outside your comfort zone. So what we want to understand is that if I'm afraid, that's a good thing.

When you push past your comfort zone despite the fear, fear lessens its grip on you, and your courage expands.

The word courage comes from the French word *coeur*, which means "heart." When you go ahead and do something despite the fear you feel, courage arises from within your heart. This is how you acquire courage. It's not the other way around, where you have to find the courage before you act. Courage comes from performing fearful acts! As you build courage you'll find that things you once thought were scary don't seem as scary at all.

LAYNE BEACHLEY

If you have the courage to set a goal and then the conviction to pursue it and achieve it, you will step outside of your comfort zone every day. So it is a necessary part of success to be willing and courageous enough to step outside of your comfort zone.

MASTIN KIPP

There's a great book called Feel The Fear and Do It Anyway. *I read the title, and that's all that I read. I didn't need to read the rest of the book. I got it. And that's really the best advice.*

MICHAEL ACTON SMITH

Things still scare me. Giving a speech in front of hundreds of people is scary. Meeting someone for the first time that you respect is scary. But you only really progress and evolve and get closer to your ultimate dreams by putting yourselves in these fearful situations. Was it Eleanor Roosevelt who said, "Do one thing every day that scares you"? I just love that philosophy.

Preparation lessens your fear. You can easily understand that the more prepared you are before a test, exam, or speech, the less fear you will have. Well, when you prepare your mind for something you're about to undertake by visualizing the outcome, you will reduce the fear you feel. You might also discover that the moment you begin to do the fearful thing, the fear disappears immediately. I have found this to be true in my life over and over again; the fear of doing something is much worse than the reality of doing it. And when you've been practicing visualization, your final reward will be the outcome turning out exactly the way you pictured it.

Taking Risks

When we made *The Secret* film, I put my career, my company, home, reputation, and everything I had worked for on the line. But not once did I consider it a risk. I knew my dream would come true.

G. M. Rao

I did put everything on the line to achieve my dream. After all, it was an investment twenty-five times more than what I had. But I never thought I would not achieve my dreams. I have always worked from the mind-set of abundance.

Michael Acton Smith

Risk is very important. Not wild and reckless risk, but making bets where you don't know what the outcome is going to be but you're more confident than not that it's going to work. My philosophy in business is to make small bets, and if something works we do more of it, and if it doesn't we dust ourselves off and go back to the drawing board.

Anastasia Soare

Of course it's scary, but I am a risk taker. If you do not take risks in life, number one, you would never find out how strong you are. Number two, you would never grow.

There will be certain times on the Hero's Journey when you're called upon to take a risk. If you're scared but you feel it's the right step to take, go ahead and take it. However, if you're scared and in doubt about it being the right step, don't take it – until you feel more sure about which way to go. When in doubt, don't act.

Pete Carroll

I was at USC and I had the time of my life there for nine years. We had won on a pretty big scale and set a lot of records. Then I was faced with an opportunity to go to the NFL and leave the best times that I'd ever had. That was the greatest risk I ever took, because I had it going on, I had it made, but this was just such an extraordinary opportunity to compete and accomplish something when the stakes were even higher and the challenges were even greater.

Grateful Heart

G. M. RAO

Gratitude is the key to reaching your dream – gratitude for what one has and what will soon come. It is the first step towards positive thinking, a feeling of "all is well with the world" that enables us to receive the blessings of the Universe.

Gratitude is essential on the Hero's Journey. It's a quiet, unassuming quality, but an immensely powerful one. The way to smooth but also to accelerate your Hero's Journey, and to experience miraculous circumstances that seem to come out of nowhere and fall into your lap, is with gratitude.

LAYNE BEACHLEY

I'm a big believer in gratitude because it puts everything into perspective, and it enables you to be in the moment. It's amazing how when you're grateful the Universe continues to provide you with more happiness and gratitude.

ANASTASIA SOARE

Wake in the morning and count your blessings that you are healthy, you can walk, you can see, you can breathe.

You can lessen and actually dissolve all manner of seemingly negative situations, like challenges, obstacles, and problems, through gratitude. If you're facing a problem, or you've hit a dead end and you can't see any way out, the act of deep gratitude will clear the way. It's as though your gratitude causes the Universe to issue a "free pass" that enables you to jump over the obstacle. Suddenly you find the obstacle you were facing diminishes or disappears and your way ahead is made clear, or you find the solution and with it the obstacle is overcome.

PETER FOYO

Gratitude has to be on the forefront of everything you do. You have to be very grateful, number one, for being here. If you have any positive things in your life, be grateful for them and they multiply. The more grateful you are the more things multiply, and the more people, events, and situations that are not that wonderful for you dissipate, disappear, or vanish. It's amazing how much more quickly things that are not to your favor vaporize the more grateful you are. I am a witness to this countless times on all levels.

If you instill yourself with a grateful heart from the beginning of your journey, and you maintain your gratitude along the way, you will make your journey that much easier, and any difficulties will be reduced dramatically. Without gratitude, you pass up the opportunity to have the Universe plot and plan and provide the right people and the exact circumstances you need to help make your dream come true in the most magical way. Instead, you're going to have a heck of a rocky ride, and in addition, you miss out on the blissful feeling that comes with a grateful heart.

MASTIN KIPP

What's so great about gratitude is that it gets you outside of yourself. You focus on what you have, you focus on blessings, you focus on other people, and that's ultimately where fulfillment comes from. When you're grateful you're not focusing on you. It stops the misery of me.

MICHAEL ACTON SMITH

The reverse is true as well. If you dwell on the negative, the problems, and the issues, you spiral down and down and just make yourself even more tense, upset, and unhappy.

MASTIN KIPP

Gratitude is essential for fulfillment. I know plenty of people who are "successful" but not grateful, and I would not want their lives.

PETER FOYO

I believe gratitude is a state of mind that has to be constantly maintained. I don't believe — I know. I know this for a fact.

In any given moment that I haven't maintained my level of gratitude, I clearly see a difference.

MICHAEL ACTON SMITH

When I'm having a down day or a bad day, if I'm sitting in my bath at the end of the day or having a coffee, I go through the things I'm grateful for – my health, my friends, my family. It suddenly lifts your mood. And I think most successful people understand that.

When we were making *The Secret* film, I never got out of bed in the morning until I had done ten to fifteen minutes of gratitude.

PETER FOYO

Even my password on my computer is one that reminds me every day of how grateful and happy I am for all the things that I have.

PETER BURWASH

One of the most important things that I got from my mom was that on Christmas Day, starting when I was five and could write, I could not go outside and play until I wrote thank-you notes to everybody who gave me a present. To this day I still try to handwrite a thank-you note to someone every single day.

LAYNE BEACHLEY

I was surfing in Noosa about a month ago, and the waves were so beautiful and the ocean felt so warm and silky, I felt so nurtured and I was having so much fun that I stopped in my tracks with this amazing sense of gratitude coming from my heart, and I just looked out to sea and thought, "This has been so much fun." All of a sudden a wave just popped up out of nowhere with no one on either side of me to challenge me for it, and I paddled into it and rode it, and it was the longest and best wave I've ever had in my life. At the end I just looked back at the ocean and I said, "Thank you."

You will never know the power of gratitude to transform your entire life until you have a grateful heart. And those who've found gratitude will sing its praises in the hope that everyone will hear.

LIZ MURRAY

After burying my mother I went to my friend's house, and I sat down in his living room. My friend Bobby started complaining because his mother burned his pork chops that she cooked for dinner. My other friend was complaining about her boss at her job, and my other friend about dropping out of school. I looked at them and I thought of mom and the pine box, and I looked at myself, and I started to realize how lucky we were. Really how blessed. Because we had our health. We were alive. I believe gratitude is nothing more than realizing that every single thing you have you could just as easily not have. And everything came into focus. I saw my wealth, because I was not only alive and healthy and young, but I had these great friends. We weren't perfect, but we loved each other. There were nights I could sleep on their couches and their floors. I did sleep in the park and the hallway a lot, but I wasn't going to die. If you think of everybody on the planet and what they go through, my concept of poverty couldn't even compare to many. I didn't have a place to live, I didn't have anything to eat, but I realized my own privilege.

PETER BURWASH

I spent six years studying leaders around the world, and 99.9 percent of them said intuition is more important than logic. Logic is what you've learned. Intuition is who you are. It doesn't mean that you can't be practical and use logic and common sense, but that first emotional feeling is very, very important.

"Have the courage to follow your heart and intuition. They somehow already know what you truly want to become."

Steve Jobs

Cofounder of Apple Inc.

MASTIN KIPP

Intuition is the primary tool you need to make your dream a reality. Without trusting your intuition, you're going to fall flat over and over again.

Intuition is a flash of knowledge that comes with a very strong and compelling feeling when we receive it. The feeling urges us to go a particular way with something happening in our lives, or sometimes to not go a particular way. While the feeling is always immediate and strong, people often second-guess the incredible communication they've received, and allow their conscious mind to talk themselves out of listening to it.

MICHAEL ACTON SMITH

I am a big believer in gut instinct. A lot of people see it as just mumbo jumbo and nonsense with no data to back it up, but I believe there must be something there because our subconscious picks up on so much more than our conscious brain, and the way the subconscious speaks to us is through our gut. When you have a feeling about someone or a situation, it is very, very important to listen to that. From my experience it's paid off far more often than it hasn't.

While science hasn't yet discovered what our intuition is or where it comes from, in ancient teachings it's revealed that intuition is knowledge that comes from a higher level of consciousness called the Universal Mind. The knowledge is transmitted through vibrations to our subconscious mind. The vibrations are then transmitted to the brain and to particular endocrine glands in our body, which interpret the knowledge in a way that we will understand. This explains why when we get an intuitive impulse it comes as an impression or a feeling in our stomach or around our heart.

Put simply, your intuition is communication from the Universe. From the perspective of the Universal Mind, what's ahead can be seen exactly, and the Universe is inspiring you to follow a particular path. Don't second-guess the communication when you receive it. No matter what evidence there is to the contrary, trust in your intuition, because the Universe knows the way.

JOHN PAUL DEJORIA
I hire people mainly off intuition – how I feel about them. If I'm in a business situation and I want to consider doing business with somebody I go for intuition, because the soul feels.

LAYNE BEACHLEY
We underestimate the value of our intuition. We fail to trust in our instincts. When I've made some of my biggest mistakes it's because I haven't listened to my intuition, or I've listened and I've questioned it. It's important that you learn to trust in it.

You might have unknowingly shut down your intuition, as many of us have, but you can reawaken your intuitive abilities. It's the very use of our intuition that strengthens it, which is the reason why you hear successful people place so much importance on it. They trusted in their intuition, followed it and acted on it, and by so doing their intuitive abilities expanded enormously. The majority of successful people use their intuition with almost every decision they make.

LAIRD HAMILTON

Whenever I have an instinct, I act on it. What's interesting is that as you become conscious of acting on it, you become better at it. It's actually a life skill that you can get better at.

Outside of just trusting in your intuition and following it more often, there's an easy way to increase your intuitive abilities. Ask questions!

When you ask a question you "receive" the answer through your intuition. You can start with easy questions where you know you will see the confirmation of the answer quickly, like, "What time will a person arrive?" Or, "What color clothing is a particular person going to be wearing today?" When your phone rings, and it's not in front of you, ask, "Who's calling me?" Sometimes your own mind will try and give you the answer, but if you can keep your own mind still when you ask the question so your mind is in receiving mode, with practice the name of the person calling will flash into your mind.

Asking a question or for a solution uses the very same process as when the answer is transmitted to you, but in reverse; your question is transmitted outward to the Universal Mind. Perhaps you will now understand how it is that when entrepreneurs ask for the perfect idea that the world needs at that time they receive an idea that ends up being *exactly* what the world needs at that time!

As you improve your intuition, you'll start to get more and more intuitive urges and inspirations to do particular things, and when they prove to be correct, like many successful people you will trust in your intuition and know it to be one of your most powerful abilities.

The Way of the Hero

The Golden Rule

LAIRD HAMILTON
You could say to my mother, "I'm on the cover of this magazine, or I did this achievement," and she'd say, "Great. But how are you treating people?"

PETER FOYO
Treat others as you wish for them to treat you. Do unto others as you wish them to do unto you.

If we didn't experience the consequences of our actions, whether those consequences were positive or negative, we'd never learn anything and we'd never evolve. You understand there's a consequence to touching a hot iron, to sleeping in on a workday, or to not paying your phone bill. But what many people don't know is that the biggest consequences we experience are due to the way we treat other people.

PETE CARROLL

The way we treat other people in life is crucially important. One of the principles in our program is that we respect everyone. A really good practice is to take into account how you treat everyone around you; that will lead you best where you want to go.

JOHN PAUL DEJORIA

Not being nice to people around you is not helpful at all. A lot of times you think you're a nice person, but you're not. Don't be mean to people. That'll hinder you. It's a golden rule – do unto others as you would have others do unto you.

"It's nice to be important, but it's more important to be nice."

Roger Federer

Tennis Champion

You can never find true happiness if you treat other people badly. We're all connected; we're part of the one family, and the Universe is for *all* of us. If we harm another person in effect we're doing it to the Universe. Big mistake… big!

Michael Acton Smith

It just feels like the right thing to do – the right way to go through life. Saying please and thank you, respecting other people, supporting others wherever you can. It's very important.

John Paul DeJoria

Next thing would be, don't spread rumors. You don't know the whole truth about something. And it's just not a good frequency to put out to the planet. Put out positive frequencies. You put out negative ones it's going to slow you and everything around you down.

If you gave a person a gift and they were rude, didn't say thank you, and were unappreciative of your gesture, you wouldn't buy another gift for that person. Well, likewise we will not be bestowed with life's gifts of good fortune, "lucky breaks," and great opportunities if we're rude, ungrateful, or mean to other human beings. If you treat people kindly, no matter what the circumstances, the Universe will return the kindness to you. It's simply the way life works for every one of us.

Laird Hamilton

It's an amazing thing: as you give and so are you generous, so will you be given to and so will generosity be given unto you. You tell people that, and it's almost too simple of a thought for them to comprehend.

LAYNE BEACHLEY

Be aware of the fact that every choice you make, every word you speak, every action you do, has a consequence and an impact on others.

PAUL ORFALEA

I believe in karma. What you put out to the world will come back to you. In other words, do good deeds. And always pay your taxes.

"Newton's third law [of motion] or karma – however each of us chooses to name it – is something I've been aware of for years. I call it cause and effect: The energy that you put into the world comes back. In other words, the fruit is in the seed. You can't sow an apple seed and expect to get an avocado tree. The consequences of your life are sown in what you do and how you behave."

Tom Shadyac

Film Director

PETER BURWASH

There are a lot of people who say, "I don't believe in karma." Well, it's not whether you believe or not. It's going to happen.

The further you go on the Hero's Journey, the more you grow and the more your mind expands. Your mind will expand to such an extent that you begin to perceive things beyond everyday living, that you never saw before. You see that if you do something good or kind for someone else, something fantastic happens for *you*. And you see that if you behave badly toward someone else, something untoward happens to *you*. You start to perceive how life works through observing the results of the actions of yourself and others around you. You can see the patterns, you can see the inner workings, you can see life's rhythms, and where you were once in the dark, now you are beginning to see everything clearly.

LAIRD HAMILTON

One thing I've been blessed with is what I call instant karma. If I say some snotty thing I'll go right out and stub my toe or hit my head. I have this instantaneous payment for negativity. It reminds me to be positive and say nice things, because I get an instant payment. I've had multiple times where I've gone out in the ocean and done something or said something to somebody that wasn't the most positive, and then I just get absolutely annihilated by a wave. And then I go out there positive and generous and polite, and I get blessed with great rides.

G. M. RAO

My purpose of doing business is not confined to financial gains. I believe there is a higher purpose I must fulfill as my karma, by making an enduring impact to society. Business is

*service to society, and the prosperity of any business will be
in proportion to the value delivered to society.*

You already know that you don't feel joyous or happy when
you speak badly of another person. That awful feeling is telling
you that behavior is far from the hero within you. And there are
consequences to that behavior, with our mental and physical
health, and our happiness.

ANASTASIA SOARE

*I don't want to do things that I know will hurt people for one
reason — because of me. Because I will get so upset and it will
eat me inside so bad that it's not worth it for me. I am more
harmed than they are harmed. And if I can do something
good, I will do it and I don't need anything in exchange.*

"When you do a loving thing, when you put out positive
energy, you feel happy. This is how human beings are
wired. So the goal of karma – if there is a goal – is not
to put out positive energy in order to get some positive
energy back. The goal is to put out positive energy and
feel positive about your life. That's where the work is.
That's why the true revolution is a personal revolution."

Tom Shadyac

Film Director

Humility

Layne Beachley
If you're on a Hero's Journey, it's really important to maintain a sense of groundedness and humility.

Peter Burwash
Become genuinely humble. Because if you're humble you're going to listen, if you listen you're going to learn, and if you learn you can teach.

Mastin Kipp
My teacher told me that the higher you go the more humble you must be. He said humility is to always remain approachable. Just because you're successful today, you have a bestseller today, doesn't mean that that success is guaranteed.

Paul Orfalea
My dad would always tell me that the biggest reason you will fail is because your past success went to your head.

Whether we go the way of the hero is decided by our behavior and the way we treat others. The hero is kind and humble, and so the way of the hero is one of kindness and humility. Our behavior will either be stepping-stones that propel us forward on our journey to our dream, or stepping-stones that take us backward. The choice is ours.

COMMITMENT

Commitment

ANASTASIA SOARE

It was my intention, my commitment, that even if a door was closed I would bang on it, I would break the door, or I would get in through the window. There was no way that I would not make that happen.

You automatically commit to something if you really want it enough. You don't even have to think about it, you just jump right into it. If there's a movie you're desperate to see, it takes no effort for you to commit to go to a theatre and see it. When you fall head over heels in love, you can't stop yourself from committing to see the other person.

LAIRD HAMILTON

The one thing about the activities we pursue on the ocean is they're very committed. You don't kind of ride a wave; you either ride it or you don't. Every wave and every ride is a belief and a commitment. You're taking that leap.

Laird Hamilton knows about commitment. If you need inspiration to strengthen your commitment, then watch a video of Laird Hamilton committing to ride one of the world's deadliest waves at Teahupo'o on the southwest coast of Tahiti.

Renowned as the heaviest wave in the world, Teahupo'o produces consistent barreling waves as high as 21 feet (6.4 meters) and as thick as a building, breaking over an extremely shallow and razor-sharp reef. The only way to surf Teahupo'o when it is that big is to be towed out on the back of a Jet Ski and released at speed.

It was not until Laird had let go of the towrope that he saw the magnitude of the double-walled monstrous wave rising up behind him. He had to make a split-second decision whether to commit to ride the wave, or not. Had Laird not made the commitment to ride the wave, it's unlikely he would have survived the mountain of water and the treacherous reef below. Instead, Laird Hamilton broke the boundaries of what is possible, and made surfing history.

LIZ MURRAY

There's something about deciding that whatever you have at the moment is enough to do whatever it is you need to do. If you always think you're missing one more thing, if you

think, "I have to have this in order to, in order to," you're
waiting for the right time. There is no right time.

The right time is never in the future. It is now. And your full
commitment is the cue that opens the doors to your dream.
It will never happen the other way around. Until you make a
commitment, you will only see walls.

MICHAEL ACTON SMITH
You have to really commit. You can't do it halfheartedly.
When you really commit, every sinew in your body, your
subconscious mind, and your conscious mind, whether
you're awake or dreaming, is working toward whatever you
are trying to achieve. And that makes all the difference.

LAIRD HAMILTON
When you commit, situations arrive for you. I'd like to go,
"I'm so smart, I thought of this," but no one's that smart.
Those things were provided because you committed to the
belief that it was possible.

LAYNE BEACHLEY
All of a sudden you're presented with guides, and the
Universe provides. It's just like the great saying, when the
student is ready the teacher will appear.

MASTIN KIPP

If you make a full commitment to your dream, doors will open. I actually think that doors have always been there, but when you fully commit you see them.

G. M. RAO

Doors opened when my commitment became a surety. I can quote the instance when we bid for the Delhi Airport. We set out to build the world's best airport. This was our dream. The project attracted the world's best and the biggest airport developers, and the bidding process was highly complex and exhaustive. We prepared ourselves with some of the most competent partners, very knowledgeable experts, and a very motivated bidding team. We visited modern airports across the world and learned from them. We overcame every obstacle in the way and emerged as the only technically qualified bidder. But our journey did not end there. The bidding process had to overcome legal challenges, which went up to the highest court of the country. The resulting delays made the stiff timelines even worse. It was to be the fifth-largest airport in the world and an extremely complicated environment with fifty-eight departments to coordinate with. Once we started the project, things fell in place, nearly $2.5 billion was raised in financing, and more than 40,000 workmen and engineers from over twenty-seven countries came together to finish the project in a world record time of thirty-seven months. The Universe blessed our commitment and dream to build the best airport in the world and *smoothed the path to achieve our goal. Today we are the fourth best among 199 airports.*

When we see someone follow their dream, we can get the mistaken idea that they must have had privileges to be able to do it. In fact, it happens the other way around; it's when you decide to take the leap into the Hero's Journey that the privileges come. When you commit to your dream, it's as though any person who can help you with your dream is summoned by the Universe to be right there for you with everything you need at the exact time you need it.

Commitment and the Universe

My daughter's boyfriend had a secure and safe job, and he knew if he worked really hard in his job over fifteen years, he would gradually climb the corporate ladder within the organization. But this job was far from his bliss. He did work really hard, but only so that he could do what he loves to do more than anything else in the world, which is surfing. So this young adult made a big decision. He decided he was going to follow his bliss.

Over several months he laid down plans to leave the corporate world and begin his dream of shaping surfboards. True to his word, he resigned on the exact day he had committed himself to. With nothing but a dream, and his commitment to it, here's what the Universe lined up for him.

A successful local shaper let him come and watch him shape surfboards. He was given free shaping lessons from another shaper, who showed him how to make some shaping tools to save even more money. A graphic designer helped him with his logo for his new business free of charge. A surf supply store gave him wholesale prices on items he needed. He was given equipment, lights, and shelving from his dad to set up his shaping studio; and he was offered free rent on a space to set up his studio, which has the most breathtaking views of the ocean and California coast that anyone could dream of having. And wherever he goes, people are asking him to shape a surfboard for them.

All of this happened in just *two* weeks. That's the summoning power of the Universe when you make a commitment to your dream, and the "privileges" that will rain down upon you when you follow your bliss.

MASTIN KIPP

If you have a dream, do not make a plan B. Will Smith said that if you have a plan B you're going to end up at plan B. You need to be all in on plan A. All your love, all your faith, all your energy, all your determination.

LAIRD HAMILTON

You have a backup plan; you know that no matter what, if only my pinky works, I can still pull something off. But it's not one you're going to use. And if you start to focus on it, then it will become your plan.

You can give yourself a reassuring safety net in your mind by knowing that no matter what happens you'll be all right, but if you seriously create a plan B you risk that being the plan that your subconscious mind materializes. Give all of your attention and focus to plan A, and that will be what materializes!

Determination

LAIRD HAMILTON
You have to be undeterred and relentless in your pursuit of your dream.

G. M. RAO
Once I made a commitment the determination to make it succeed was born.

PETE CARROLL
Not everybody has the same level of determination. When the obstacle shows up and the doubts start to creep in, not everybody has the same grit that drives them to stick to it. But the potential is there.

When you tried to walk as a baby, you fell down hundreds of times. When you first tried to feed yourself, you put the food in your eye, on your cheek, and everywhere but your mouth. Learning how to talk was a long journey full of mistakes, but you never once considered giving up. Determination is part of your very nature. You have it within you, and you can find it again.

Michael Acton Smith

By real bootstrapping we managed to cobble together the cash to get the business going. But it's tough. Banks won't lend you money. No one is willing to take a risk on you if you've never done anything before. You just have to roll your sleeves up and find a way.

If you have a burning desire for your dream, then you will have all the determination you need to make it a reality. There may be days when you feel a bit down, there may be days when you doubt yourself, or when you even feel you can't do it, but your burning desire will carry you through those days. A burning desire within you is a powerful force that overrides any temporary feeling of wanting to give up, and provides you with a commitment and a determination that cuts through any difficulty you may encounter. When we were making *The Secret* film my burning desire and belief were so great that I never even thought about acquiring determination because my strong desire meant I was already filled with it.

Anastasia Soare

I needed a credit card. I went to the bank, and they didn't want to give me a credit card because I didn't have a history,

*and my mother didn't have a history. I said to the Wells
Fargo bank manager in Beverly Hills, "If you do not help me,
how will I build credit? Give me $500. I'm not asking you
for $5 million. I will put $1,000 in the bank and you give me
$500." He didn't want to. I said, "Listen, I'm going to set
myself on fire in front of the bank." So he gave me the $500
credit card. And I'm still a customer of Wells Fargo.*

Determination also arises out of your belief in yourself. When you
believe in yourself you naturally have determination. Coaches
and personal trainers have a positive impact on us because they
continually tell us that we can be better, that we can do it, and
they urge us on at every step. Their belief in us makes us believe
we can achieve our dream, and when we believe, we have the
determination to achieve anything. You can be your own coach!
You can urge yourself on with positive self-talk; tell yourself you
can do it, that you've triumphed in far tougher times, that you've
got what it takes, that you made a commitment and the success of
your dream is in your hands, and that you *will* be victorious! Your
subconscious mind will hear every word you say, and then you
will do it!

MASTIN KIPP

*Dreams are like a seed; it takes time to plant it. It doesn't
happen overnight. We've forgotten that we have to earn it.
We're in this instant gratification, give it to me now, and by
the way, I don't have to do anything for it, just give it to me.*

And dreams are earned. They're earned. If it hasn't happened yet, keep trying.

Never, Never, Never Give Up

LAIRD HAMILTON
It's too easy just to give up. Giving up is a cop-out. To go, "I'm old, I'm this, I'm that." That's just a disclaimer to not really put out the effort.

PETE CARROLL
If you feel like you're done, then you are, because that's hopeless. We don't want to ever get to the point where we're totally hopeless. There is always hope. To me, something good is always going to come your way.

LIZ MURRAY
Even if you get a rush of determination, you can still encounter a day where you want to give up. I got rejected quite a bit, to the point of almost depression. On one particular day, I'd been rejected for the millionth time, and I'm crossing off these schools and I'm getting to the bottom of the list, and I'm running out of any schools that would take me. I came to one moment where I had to make a choice. In my pocket I had enough money to either take the subway and go to the next school interview, or I could give up right there and I could go get a slice of pizza. Pizza or interview...

which one? I just felt, "I'm homeless and hungry. They're going to reject me." All of a sudden the part of me that dreams thought, "What if that's the school that lets me in?" I had to ditch the idea of the pizza and get on the subway and go to the school. And that was the school that let me in – that very next school. You never know when you're about an inch away. You have to do it one more time. Even if the one more time didn't work, then do it one more time.

You live in a world of duality, and so there are going to be both ups and downs. You will have experienced those days when for whatever reason you feel really down, and every simple thing feels like an effort, as though you're wading through mud with every step. On those days you probably didn't feel like you had very much or any determination.

You will also have experienced those days when you feel incredibly happy and energized, when you feel on top of the world, and like you can achieve anything. Well, that joyful, blissful feeling is one of the highest and most powerful human emotions you have, because with it you not only feel invincible, you *are* invincible. When you're full of joy you are also full of determination, because from the perspective of joy, everything seems easy. Seek your joy – follow your bliss – and you will find all the determination you need to achieve your dream.

Part Three
THE QUEST

THE LABYRINTH

The Labyrinth

LAIRD HAMILTON

The journey itself will never be as you think. You have an idea of the destination, but you never know the route.

Many people give up on their dreams or don't even begin to pursue them because from where they are standing they can't see the whole path to their dream. You will never see the whole path ahead, and so you will never know how your dream is going to come true. No successful person has ever known *how* his or her dream would happen. They simply believed that it would happen, and did not give up until it had.

MASTIN KIPP

I never thought my life would look like it does now. I knew it would feel this way, but I never knew it would be this way.

The path to your dreams is like being in a labyrinth. All you can see is the next few feet ahead of you. You can't see what's around the next turn until you go around it, and then you see the next few feet after that. Sometimes there are dead ends and you have to turn back, and sometimes there are shortcuts that you stumble upon as if by magic and which accelerate your passage. The path to your dreams unfolds in exactly the same way.

LAYNE BEACHLEY
No one can see the whole way. You've just got to be willing to put your first foot forward and go on that journey.

MASTIN KIPP
The process of living your dreams is all about the adventure – to see what's next. No one you look up to, no person who inspires you, started a journey with a certain outcome. They may have had an idea, intention, or end goal, but they had no idea how they were going to get there.

Being in a labyrinth is the very adventure you wanted to have. You didn't want to see everything, know everything ahead, and be able to make your dreams come true with a snap of your fingers. You wanted the challenge of the journey, because only through overcoming the challenges would you have the real happiness and fulfillment that every human being is searching for.

ANASTASIA SOARE
There are things that will not work the way you put it down, and you have to be prepared through your strategy to change – to take another road. It's like a labyrinth. You go and you find a dead-end. Well, you turn back and you find another one. But it will still take you to point Z to finish your dream.

When you are on the path to your dreams, a wall might suddenly appear, and you feel like you've hit a dead end and you're finished. But just like being in a labyrinth, no matter how things appear, there is always another path you can take. When you know that the success of your dream is at the center of the labyrinth, you will not be in the least bit daunted by any unexpected twists and turns, because you will know that your success could be around the very next corner. And that's exactly how dreams come true.

JOHN PAUL DEJORIA
Realize that it may not come all at one time, but if you really want something it's a cinch by the inch, it's hard by the yard. Little steps along the way.

LIZ MURRAY
I understand people are up against a lot. But even in circumstances of great constraint you can still do one thing. It's like that Theodore Roosevelt quote, "Do what you can, with what you have, where you are." You can pick one thing and dedicate yourself to that, and even if it takes a long time,

inch by inch and choice by choice you will carve out a new life for yourself. It doesn't have to be the Hollywood, turn-on-a-dime, dramatic thing that happens.

One Step at a Time

Along your journey, remind yourself that one step at a time is all you need to take. One step at a time is all you can *ever* take. And no matter where you find yourself or in what situation, you can always take one step. You can make yourself feel overwhelmed if you let your mind get carried away with all of the possibilities of what could be ahead. The path to your dream will never unfold in the way you think anyway, so just keep bringing yourself back to "one step at a time." Those words helped me enormously when we were making *The Secret* film. When my dream seemed to be going way off the path that my human mind thought it should take, I brought myself back to just taking the next step, and by taking one step at a time, my dream came true.

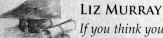

LIZ MURRAY

If you think you can see every step you're mistaken. That's the mistake we make thinking we need to – or even that we could – control everything. My mother went to Narcotics Anonymous, and all these people do the serenity prayer: "God, grant me the serenity to accept the things I cannot change, the courage to change the things I can, and the wisdom to know the difference." And that is everything.

*I couldn't bring my mother back. I could not change my
father's HIV diagnosis. I couldn't control the weather. You
could make a list of all the things you can't control, and if
you put your energy into those it'll go to the wind. Instead,
you say, "Okay, what can I do?"*

MICHAEL ACTON SMITH
*I have been taking one step at a time and occasionally
stepped backward or hit dead ends, but as long as you've got
that big vision in mind and you believe you will get there,
eventually you do.*

And, just like being in a labyrinth, one day you turn a corner, and
suddenly you've arrived; just like that your dream has come true.

Once you have achieved your dream and you are looking back
on the journey you took, you will realize that every wall forced
you to take an alternate path, which led you not only to your
dream, but often a far better version of your dream than you ever
thought was possible. In fact, there are no walls; there is only
the *appearance* of walls. There are no dead ends; there is only the
appearance of dead ends. Both are actually only detours for the
purpose of redirecting you to that greater version of your dream.

G. M. RAO
*In my journey of four decades, it happened a number of times
that things did not turn out the way we had anticipated. I did
not hesitate to stop and change course with an open mind.*

We experienced this recently when we acquired 50 percent of an international energy giant for over $1.2 billion. When things were not turning out the way we anticipated and our aspirations were not in congruence with our partners, we decided to opt out even if it meant facing a temporary setback. However, in hindsight and subsequently we have more than made up. If the purity of intention is there, the Universe finds a way to reward you.

If your commitment begins to waver at any time on the Hero's Journey, through disappointment, rejection, or something that didn't go the way you thought it would go, those are the times when you need to remind yourself that you are always being moved to your dream in the way that will bring about the greatest outcome.

Mastin Kipp

As an entrepreneur, there's a term called pivoting, and pivoting basically means if it doesn't work I'm going to pivot – implement what I learned and come up with something new. And that's really what the Hero's Journey is all about. See what works, change what doesn't, try again, and ultimately you'll get there.

John Paul DeJoria

Dreams change. When I started John Paul Mitchell Systems back in 1980 with my partner, the dream was, "If we could do $5 million a year we'd each make $200,000 to $250,000.

We'd be set for life." Well, when we got to that point with the size of our company, our dream changed and grew bigger. So it's important to know that once you achieve that dream you go on to another dream. It's an evolution.

There is one thing you can count on when you follow your dream through the thrilling twists and turns of your Hero's Journey. Your dream will never end up being smaller than what you thought. It will only become greater, in ways you could never have imagined.

NAYSAYERS AND ALLIES

Naysayers & Allies

PETER FOYO

We all encounter naysayers. To build a business this size, I've had to compete with the biggest naysayers.

Peter Foyo had to face naysaying from every direction, from potential investors, competitors, and government officials that could have prevented him from achieving his dream. But despite all of the naysayers and all of the difficulties that stood in his path, today Nextel Mexico has a workforce of 17,000 people servicing over 4 million customers with the latest in telecommunications. From his beginnings as a child of hardworking immigrants, Peter achieved his enormous dream for Nextel in less than five years, and when he was only thirty-eight years of age. With Peter at the helm, Nextel Mexico has continued to grow rapidly over the last ten years into a multibillion-dollar company.

MASTIN KIPP

Naysayers are part of the journey. Recognize that if you're successful, if you're doing something great, people are going to love you and some people are going to hate you. I just see that as a sign of success.

Every person who has ever done something that had never been done before faced hundreds and hundreds of naysayers who said their dream was impossible. What do you think people said to Edison when he said he was going to invent a device that would light up an entire room? What do you think people said to Alexander Graham Bell when he told people he was inventing an instrument that would enable two people to talk to each other from thousands of miles apart? You can trust in the fact that if you have a big dream and there are lots of naysayers around, they're the proof that you *can* do it!

ANASTASIA SOARE

By 1995, I was so busy that I thought, "I have to open my store in Beverly Hills." I went to the landlord and he said to me, "Are you out of your mind? You can't make money to pay rent doing eyebrows." He didn't want to rent me the space. But he saw that I was so crazy and he committed. He said, "Okay, I will give you six months." Well, the first week there was a line outside the store and he called me one day and said, "I have never seen anything like this. Are you sure you are doing eyebrows there?"

Laird Hamilton

Naysayers are always present. And as a sensitive being, you're always going to be affected by it; it's just what you do with that. Don't fall the victim to it because then they have achieved their goal.

The effect naysayers have is up to *you.* Only you choose how you react to them. If you allow one naysayer to get to you you'll open yourself up to being affected by more naysayers, so don't let them bother you. It's the complete opposite of what the naysayers intended, but instead of deterring you, their words can even inspire you with a renewed energy that propels and drives you to achieve your dream.

Peter Foyo

It's a spectacular feeling to take a naysayer as a propelling factor of success. They actually push you faster to be happier and to be more successful.

Laird Hamilton

I used a lot of the naysayers as fuel. I took "You can't do that!" As "Oh yeah, I can do that!" That just drove me. I just spun it on its head and turned a negative into a positive, because especially in my world the naysayers were many, and they still are.

PETER BURWASH
I was not disturbed by the criticism as much as I felt like I was going down the right path.

"So many times I have been told that it can't be done. Again and again, I've had to use every ounce of perseverance to make it happen."

Howard Schultz

Chairman and CEO of Starbucks

Naysayers can also serve to redirect you on to another, better path. You might have fixed in your mind the way you think your dream will happen, and as you follow that way, you meet with naysayers who are decision-makers, and they stop your dream in its tracks. Without being able to go any further you're forced to look for another way, and you find another way to achieve your dream that is far superior to the path you were on – thanks to the naysayers. Bless them!

PETER FOYO
When I run into people who are extremely negative, they're actually a lead into where I'm going. They direct me even faster in the right direction versus drawing me back.

PETER BURWASH
When I was playing in Canada, the president of the tennis association at the time wrote me a letter and said, "You

should give up the game because you're so bad." And rather than see that as a hurdle I saw that as a challenge. When I returned to Canada to play in the national championships, I was getting ready to change ends and serve for the final game of the match. I took out the letter where this guy says I was so bad, and yet here I was about to win the national championships.

Ignore the Trivial Many

A valuable piece of advice you might want to consider for your journey is to instill belief and conviction in yourself before you tell other people about your dream. If you start telling people about your dream too soon, you may be disheartened by their responses and give up before you've really begun. This has happened to many people before, and it could even have happened to you. You got a great idea to do something that was not within your usual expertise, you shared it with others, they filled you with doubt, and your idea and dream were shut down before you could even get them off the ground. Then, as fate would have it, some time later you discover that the great idea you once had has materialized in the world through someone else – and it became a great success.

JOHN PAUL DEJORIA
Pay attention to the vital few. Ignore the trivial many.

LIZ MURRAY

Be careful letting other people define things for you. People have their opinions and they're very quick to tell you what's possible and what's impossible. It's unfortunate the conviction that people speak with. No one knows what's possible until they're already doing it. No one.

"Keep away from people who try to belittle your ambitions. Small people always do that, but the really great make you feel that you, too, can become great."

Mark Twain

Author

When I decided to make *The Secret*, I didn't tell another person about my dream until I had it fully formulated in my mind. I spent four months researching, planning, and integrating it within me, until I knew no one could dissuade me. Only then did I share it with others, when a thousand naysayers could have said my dream would never happen and not one of them would have affected me.

Work on your dream, work on your belief in your dream, and formulate your dream in your mind until the picture of it is crystal clear before you share it with others.

LAYNE BEACHLEY

When I was growing up surfing at Manly Beach, there would be two guys on my right telling me to get out of the water and two guys on my left saying, "We think you're great, and we enjoyed surfing with you." So who do you think I'm going to listen to? The two guys on my left, of course.

PETE CARROLL

What gave me the strength to really grow from getting fired and come out of it stronger was that I didn't sanction the decision. I just didn't accept it. I challenged the thought that they were right and I knew that there was reason to feel otherwise.

The truth about naysayers is they are often people who have closed their minds and are not living their full potential themselves. If they were living their full potential they would know from their own experience that anything is possible.

JOHN PAUL DEJORIA

When I was in the eleventh grade, in front of the whole class our business teacher told my friend Michelle and me that we would never amount to anything. We knew he was wrong. We would definitely do something with our lives. Michelle became a superstar. That's Michelle Phillips of the Mamas and the Papas.

I had many experiences with naysayers when we were making *The Secret* film, but one stands out above all the others. I was doing a presentation of the first cut of the film to a large group of television executives. It had taken a year of work and sacrificing everything I had to get to that point. And at the end of the screening the executives responded to the film with not a single compliment. Instead, they were severely critical, and found fault with every aspect of the film. I left the presentation in shock, and in a daze I wandered the streets after leaving the building where the meeting was held. Eventually I pulled myself together and headed to the airport for the one-hour flight home. On that flight I realized there was no way I could possibly resolve all of the executives' endless criticisms. And I didn't need to. By the time the plane landed I had been inspired with a few changes that could be made to the film. We followed those inspirations and put them into the film, and they were the very elements that would go on to make the film a huge success.

Allies

While you will almost certainly encounter naysayers on your Hero's Journey, you are also destined to meet many, many allies, angels already in your life or who appear, even if only briefly, to support you and help you on your journey.

MASTIN KIPP

I don't believe there's such a thing as a self-made success or a self-made person, because everybody's had help along the way.

LAYNE BEACHLEY

All successful people have achieved by standing on the shoulders of others, and it's important, no matter how successful you are, that you remember and realize who has helped you along in this journey.

No one achieves a dream on his or her own. There are untold numbers of people who will support you and go out of their way to help you on the path to your dream. Of all the experiences we have on the Hero's Journey, the surprises of people you know and those you barely know who support and help you along the way, are perhaps the most wonderful.

MICHAEL ACTON SMITH

I work with huge supporting networks. Everyone from my family, who has supported me, to investors who put money into the business, to employees who came to work for me even when ideas were just a sketch on the napkin.

LAYNE BEACHLEY

Setting an auspicious goal to become a world champion as an eight year old was obviously very challenging, and there were times when I wanted to quit and I wanted to walk away

> *and put my hands up in the air and say, "This is all just*
> *too hard." Fortunately I had individuals in my life at those*
> *poignant times who picked me up and went, "You can do*
> *this. I believe in you." And when someone who you respect*
> *and appreciate in your life tells you that they believe in you,*
> *it instills so much belief in you. It's really important that you*
> *have those people in your life.*

During the making of *The Secret* film, there were an endless number of people who came into our lives and helped us with the next step we needed to take. In addition to all of those allies, I had a team of people who worked with me to create the film, and without their dedication and support my dream would never have come true.

There was a time when I didn't have enough money to pay my team their salaries. I had mortgaged my home to the limit, taken out overdrafts, and maxed out every credit card I had to keep the production of the film going, but I reached this heartbreaking day where I did not have the money to pay my team. Do you know what they did? A couple of my senior team members got together and withdrew cash on their credit cards to pay those who couldn't survive without their salary. Without a doubt, the people in my team were my greatest allies.

THE ROAD OF TRIALS & MIRACLES

The Road of Trials & Miracles

ANASTASIA SOARE
Life is a challenge. If you think life is smooth and it's perfect, you are wrong or you are delusional.

PETER BURWASH
Every day has hurdles. There's nobody who wakes up in the morning without something wrong physically, mentally, emotionally, or spiritually. Accept the fact that you're going to have hurdles. Everybody has them. People say, "Why me?" Why not you?

"The path to your goal is not always going to be smooth. Obstacles will arise and problems will develop, but you have to remember what you're striving for... don't forget the big picture and don't let small mishaps or small failures stop you."

Derek Jeter

American Baseball Champion

Challenges and Obstacles

Every obstacle or challenge you encounter on the Hero's Journey transforms you as you acquire strength of character and the qualities and abilities you need to overcome the obstacle or challenge. The emergence of these qualities and abilities shape you into the kind of person you need to become to achieve your dream. For that reason, challenges and obstacles are great indications that you are well along the way on your Hero's Journey. In fact, the bigger the obstacles and challenges you face, the bigger your success will be, and the closer you are to achieving it.

MASTIN KIPP

The number-one thing people gain from challenges is not the stuff they get, but who they become. When you face a challenge and you overcome that challenge, you have greater faith in yourself, you have greater faith in your abilities, you have greater trust of the divine, and you can do something even bigger. Overcoming obstacles is perhaps the greatest

gift – far greater than the stuff that you get. Because that's
something that can't ever be taken from you.

PETER BURWASH
Once you go through a series of heartaches, challenges,
upside-downs, capsizing, whatever, you always come out the
better because of the tremendous self-confidence gained.

If you have ever faced anything in your life that you had no
choice but to overcome, you will have found strengths that
you didn't know you had. Those strengths you gain form your
character and transform you into someone greater than you were
before. Women who have given birth know this well. Mothers
need to be strong to raise and care for a baby. They need patience,
tolerance, determination, and physical endurance. The experience
of labor and giving birth prepares them for motherhood with the
necessary strengths and qualities to do it well. It's because of her
strength through the most difficult times that many of us consider
our mother a hero.

MASTIN KIPP
When you really step up and embrace the challenge, and
when you overcome that challenge, that part of you is like,
"Holy crap, you did it!" You can't just sit there and say, "I
love myself." Self-esteem is earned.

LAYNE BEACHLEY

Challenges and obstacles present all of us with the opportunity to grow and improve and learn, and step outside of our comfort zone and experience what life truly has to offer.

The purpose of challenges and obstacles on the Hero's Journey is to prepare us with the qualities and abilities we will need to maintain our dream when it comes true. Without having the skills to handle success, your dream would go up in a puff of smoke no sooner than it had arrived. So challenges and obstacles are preparation for our success.

G. M. RAO

The course of my journey in business has been like the flow of a river, where each obstacle made me change course, eventually to reach my destination. All my life has been full of challenges. Each challenge was a meaningful coincidence, and opened a door to a bigger opportunity.

JOHN PAUL DEJORIA

From challenges and obstacles we gain a full education, and it's part of our success. So many times in life things have happened and they didn't go the way I wanted to, but through it I realized: had I not gone through this, later on in life I wouldn't be as happy or successful as I am right now. There are things in life that are going to happen, but these will be lessons that take you on to your ultimate reward.

If I reflect back on my journey, the obstacles and challenges I faced were nothing compared to the obstacles and challenges I faced in my life before I decided to follow my dream. When you have a purpose and you're following your dream, obstacles and challenges don't seem as difficult or as hard as they do when you have no purpose at all. Without a purpose, challenges or obstacles can appear to have no reason, and simply feel like bad luck. However they do have a purpose, because you have to evolve, and so even if you try to hide from life you will still face challenges and obstacles.

PETER BURWASH
My basic philosophy has been: if something good happens I appreciate it, if something bad happens I see it as a learning process.

Challenges and obstacles are tough for all of us when we're first confronted by them, but they're only tough while you haven't found the solution and the way to overcome them. You are *never* given an obstacle or challenge that you do not have the ability to overcome. Never.

PETER FOYO
Mind-set overcomes obstacles. And my mind-set is happiness and being grateful, and it always has been that way. I also made a decision to share a lot more financially, and the more you share the more the obstacles go away.

Peter Foyo puts his success down to the use of a handful of principles that he practiced religiously to realize his dream. No obstacle he faces ever deters him. He maintains a positive and happy mind-set through constant practice of gratitude. He helps other people wherever he can. And when he is confronted with any difficulty he uses one of the hero's greatest abilities – visualization.

PETER FOYO

There have been obstacles from competitors, from corruption, from regulators, but I don't really feel them. I feel the outcome; I feel where I'm going. An obstacle is more of a detour. I say, "Okay, so how are we going to get around that?" I visualize something different.

Visualize the outcome you want, and you will receive the solution to a problem or the best way to overcome a challenge. But to hear the solution when it's given to you, your mind must be free of worried thoughts.

Imagine if you were lost and you asked someone for directions, but while the person was giving you directions and trying to help you get out of your predicament, you kept talking about how lost you were, how being lost was a big problem, how you'd been trying to find your way out, and how you're now worried that you'll never find your way out. You wouldn't be able to hear the directions, even as they were being given to you! If your mind is busy with thoughts of worry or anguish, you can't hear the solution from the Universe.

LIZ MURRAY

I would wake up sometimes sleeping on my friend's floor. I had to get to the early morning class that I signed up for before school starts, and I needed something to motivate me to get there. So I would see this runner in my mind. I guess it was supposed to be me, but I only ever saw her back. And she was running down a track by herself. I saw these physical hurdles, and she would jump the hurdles and jump the hurdles. I would lie there picturing this runner so I could get myself up to go. I would say, "Okay, you're tired, that's a hurdle. Your work, you did it last night. You jumped a hurdle. Taking the train ride down there with no breakfast, you're starving. Hurdle, hurdle, hurdle." And I would see her jumping the hurdles with her sinewy back and sweating under the sun. So every time something got in my way, what if it was just another hurdle? Because a hurdle's not separate from the track; a hurdle is part of the track, and it wouldn't be an indication that I was off my track. When things were in the way that was just part of the course, and eventually if I jumped those hurdles enough I would reach my finish line.

MICHAEL ACTON SMITH

I didn't know how, but in the darkest times, because I so believed in this product, I knew I was going to crack it. If you stay in it, and you ask the Universe – it delivers.

JOHN PAUL DEJORIA

A hindrance to anyone being successful is when there's rejection they give up. One of the keys to becoming successful at anything is to be prepared for a lot of rejection, and don't let it affect you. A lot of people aren't prepared when they start something, and they figure they're a failure and it stops them. If all these rejections didn't happen, I could never have started John Paul Mitchell Systems.

Failures & Mistakes

"We make mistakes. It wouldn't be any fun if we didn't make mistakes. If I went out and played golf and every one of the eighteen holes I hit a hole in one, I wouldn't be playing golf for very long; I mean, you have to go into the rough occasionally to make the game interesting. Not too often though."

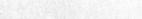

Business Magnate and Investor

LAYNE BEACHLEY

If you take the time to reflect back on some of your so-called failures and mistakes, or setbacks and disappointments, you realize they are all necessary parts of our journey.

PAUL ORFALEA

How does a baby get up and fall down? That takes a lot of guts. The whole process of going from zero to five has a lot of obstacles. But you learn from your mistakes.

LAIRD HAMILTON

You have to be willing to subject yourself to failure. I know that for me the greatest lessons come from the failures not from the successes. That's what leads us closer to our dream.

If you haven't acquired the necessary qualities of discernment or good judgment to realize your dream, failures and mistakes will ensure you develop them. You could put your trust in something because of what someone else said, and it fails. You could make a decision without thinking things through and find you've made a big mistake. When you reflect back on the failure or the mistake, however, you might see there were red flags or warning signs you ignored that were telling you something wasn't right. In other words, you ignored your intuition.

LAYNE BEACHLEY

Mistakes are really a learning opportunity, and the only mistake is not learning the lesson the first time. And the great thing about the Universe is it'll keep providing you with the same lesson until you learn it.

You might see that you needed to do your own research and not trust in other people's opinions so blindly. Or you might see that you needed to think things through more carefully before taking a big action.

> "I learned more from the one restaurant that didn't work than from all the ones that were successes."

Wolfgang Puck

Restaurateur and Businessman

G. M. RAO

We must celebrate failures, for they arise out of action and therefore become the greatest grounds for learning. And we must concentrate on that learning so that mistakes do not get repeated. To encourage new ideas, new approaches, experimentation, and innovation, a mistake should not be censured.

When you take responsibility for your failures and mistakes, without blaming anyone else, and you look for the lessons hidden within them, they become powerful tools for your advancement on the Hero's Journey. Mistakes and failures are inevitable; whether you extract the magic they contain is up to you!

LAIRD HAMILTON

There's a formulaic process. First you have to believe that it's possible. Then you have to be willing to fail; you get back up and do it again, and pretty soon you're like, "Wow, I'm going." And then, "I'm getting a little better," and then,

"I'm good at this." Pretty soon you're at the top, and then you realize it wasn't about getting to the top, it was about that process. And you get addicted to the process of it.

Miracles

PETER BURWASH
I have been very grateful for the moments that have happened, and realized that we're not that independent. We're very dependent, not just on oxygen but on good fortune, good timing, and other people.

There may be trials on the Hero's Journey, but you're also going to experience the miracles that happen along the way. In truth, the miracles far outweigh the trials. From my own experience, the magic and miracles that happened while I was on my way to my dream were *as* thrilling as the realization of my dream. When the Universe starts lining things up for you in a way that no human mind could ever do, I promise you, it will take your breath away. You will ask time and time again, "How did that happen?!"

LIZ MURRAY
I was sleeping on the streets, and I used to shoplift; not the best habit in the world, but I needed to eat. I also used to go to Barnes & Noble and shoplift self-help books, and I would read them in the stairwells. Then my story spread and I got a call from this Stephen Covey company. I went out and I

*spoke, and it took me until I was standing in front of him
to realize that I had stolen his book. I had to tell him, "I
shoplifted your book." And he told me it was on the house.*

Liz Murray was just eighteen years old when Stephen Covey
asked her to share the stage with him to tell her story. That day
proved to be a miraculous one in Liz's life, because it set her on a
path of public speaking to share her story and inspire others. Liz
went on to write her own best-selling book, and to share the stage
with people such as Mikhail Gorbachev, the Dalai Lama, and
Tony Blair.

PETER BURWASH

*At the end of 1968, when I was on the tennis tour, I didn't
have any money left. I was playing with Issy Sharp, founder
of Four Seasons Hotels, and he said, "What are you going
to do?" I said, "I don't know, maybe I'll go back to teach
school." And he said, "What do you need to stay on the
tour?" I said, "Two world air tickets at $1,800 each. That
$3,600 will allow me to stay." The next day I went down
to his office and he reached across the table with a $3,600
check and said, "Good luck." That turned my life around.
That was a very, very integral part of being able to stay on
the tour, which allowed me to get a good world ranking. And
everything else was history after that.*

MASTIN KIPP

I was couch surfing, living in an 8 x 8 feet pool house in my ex-girlfriend's parents' house. The Daily Love *was my hobby, but I had just decided to do it full time. After a month of tweeting, emailing, being all in, and dealing with massive uncertainty, Kim Kardashian tweeted to over 2 million people to follow my Twitter handle. I'll never forget that moment. Overnight we went from 1,000 to 10,000 followers. I felt the presence of the divine urging me to keep going.*

Layne Beachley's big dream was to become the world's best female surfer, and to do that she had to beat the world record of four consecutive world titles. Layne was competing in the final event of the year for her fourth world title. The athlete with the highest points accrued over several events in the year wins the world title, and going into the final event of the year Layne was leading in points and her fourth world title was within her grasp.

LAYNE BEACHLEY

It was 2001, and it was the final event of the year. I was in the quarterfinals and I fell on my last wave, which cost me the heat and which potentially cost me my fourth consecutive title. I felt like I had let the whole world down. I was so deeply devastated because my ultimate goal was to match and then beat the current record, which was four consecutive world titles.

Layne needed a miracle. Several of Layne's competitors now had an opportunity to overtake Layne's total points and claim the world title if they won the contest that day.

LAYNE BEACHLEY

Pauline Menczer, the 1993 world champion, walked past me and said, "Don't worry, we've got this covered." She wanted to see me win that world title. She went on a rampage to demolish the competition, preventing anyone the opportunity to claim the world title. Pauline went on to win the contest, and handed me my fourth consecutive world title in the process. She had really poor eyesight and couldn't afford eye correction surgery, so I decided to pay for her eye correction surgery as a thank you.

Layne Beachley went on to win six consecutive world titles.

LIZ MURRAY

When my life story was printed in the New York Times, *I learned a lot about someone being a hero. All these people from my community showed up at my school, and they were all there to help me. I didn't know them. In their arms they were carrying baked brownies, clothing out of their closets, and gift packages for college, and they were just standing there like a band of angels. I had been homeless; they paid rent on an apartment. They built beds to sleep on. They turned on the lights. They filled up the refrigerator. Everybody was wonderful in their own way, but there was this one lady. She came about three weeks after that group of people, and she immediately shook my hand in front of my school, introduced herself, and apologized to me. I asked her for what, and she said, "Because I read about you in the* New York Times, *I pinned the article on my refrigerator, and every day I tell myself I'm going to help you. But then I'm, 'Oh, no time, no money – can't do it.' Well, sweetheart, this morning I was doing my laundry and it dawned on me. Liz must have some laundry." And that's when I realized she was standing in front of this minivan. She looked at me and said, "Well, do you have some laundry?" We went and got my clothes, and she cleaned them once a week every week. She told me, "I can't do much, but I can do that." And if everybody on this planet would get that lesson – I can't do much, but I can do that. I learned that you can help other people in small ways that are available to you right this second. If we all lived that way, you would see a shift in the thinking on this planet.*

THE SUPREME ORDEAL

The Supreme Ordeal

ANASTASIA SOARE

Unless you want to wake up and do the same thing every day, you need to be a fighter. You need to be a warrior if you want to make a difference, if you want to be significant. I wanted to be significant. I wanted to do things that would change my life, and would change people's lives. I cannot be ordinary.

MICHAEL ACTON SMITH

It was tough. It took months for the business to really get going. We weren't making much money. Hardly anyone knew about the Internet back in 1998, so we had barely any customers buying our products. One of our friends would order from us every month under a fake name just to give us the bit of confidence to cheer us along to keep going. We were close to giving up.

On the Hero's Journey there is a final challenge you will face before the reward of success, and the size of that final challenge is determined by the size of your dream. This final challenge has been called the Supreme Ordeal. It can appear like the death of your dream, but when you arise out of it, your dream is born.

MICHAEL ACTON SMITH

That's the classic Hero's Journey, isn't it? Reaching a complete dead end, all hope is almost lost, and then you turn it around. It would be boring if we hit it out of the park straight away and never have to strive or struggle.

LAYNE BEACHLEY

You do have to hit rock bottom and you have to go through your challenges to bounce back up.

You will have seen the Supreme Ordeal in movies, where the hero has overcome every obstacle on his quest, and just when he's about to rescue the princess or seize the Holy Grail there is one final challenge he has to overcome to seize the ultimate prize.

MASTIN KIPP

Every hero almost dies, or does die and is reborn. And that idea, of psychological, emotional, spiritual, or physical, literal death, is terrifying for people. But we have to walk into that, like Christ on the cross, his arms wide open.

"Had I really succeeded at anything else, I might never have found the determination to succeed in the one arena where I truly belonged. I was set free, because my greatest fear had been realized, and I was still alive, and I still had a daughter whom I adored, and I had an old typewriter, and a big idea. And so rock bottom became a solid foundation on which I rebuilt my life."

J.K. Rowling

Author of the Harry Potter books

JOHN PAUL DEJORIA

I worked for a company and ran two full positions for them. Even though they were up, they said I wasn't their type of manager and fired me. I went to work for another company. After one year they fired me because I didn't hang out with them on the weekends. Next company I worked for I tripled their sales, and one day the owner of the company said, "I'm sorry, but we have to let you go because we have someone that could do your job for half the money." And then I started John Paul Mitchell Systems. Two years into John Paul Mitchell Systems I realized something; had I not worked for those three companies that fired me, it would have been virtually impossible to start John Paul Mitchell Systems, because each company taught me something. Even though I was fired, it was like the Universe was moving me on, teaching me various things along the way, whether I knew it or not.

When John Paul DeJoria and his business partner Paul Mitchell were just about to launch their hair care products, an investor who had agreed to provide money for their business suddenly withdrew all funds. John Paul and his partner were left with massive commitments, no way of paying their bills, and no way of surviving the next forty-five days until their clients paid their accounts. They appeared to be doomed. But then John Paul was struck with a brilliant idea – to offer discounts for cash payments on delivery. Almost every client took the offer, and John Paul Mitchell Systems was saved.

LAYNE BEACHLEY

In 1995, I was rated second in the world and I was in contention for my first world title. I was pushing myself quite hard, and then in 1996 I got struck down with chronic fatigue. Physically there doesn't seem to be anything wrong, but mentally, emotionally, spiritually, you've hit rock bottom. I hit rock bottom to the point where I had suicidal tendencies; for someone who was such a lover of life, it was really disconcerting. I wanted to quit, but I still had something to live for; I chose to focus on my love of surfing. I didn't have the physical strength to do that thing I love, but I now had the mental strength to work toward doing it again. I committed to going to Hawaii to compete even though I knew I didn't have the strength to do so. I thought, "I'm just going to go over there and enjoy it." I won every event in Hawaii that year, and that was the year before I won my first world title. That experience of chronic fatigue was a really valuable lesson. I'm really glad I didn't give up.

PETE CARROLL

Through the course of my coaching I had been fired a few times. When you get fired in my business everybody in the sporting world knows about it. It's in the newspaper. It's on the news. It's a big deal. It's not like you get fired and you have to go home and just deal with your wife. You have to deal with everybody else. It's a tremendous challenge. But okay, this happened, and there must be something in this that's going to help me be better and stronger down the road. That's where the epiphany hit, that I had worked a long time but I hadn't dug deep enough to really get in touch with what was important to me so I could bring it out in my next program. My back was to the wall and I didn't know if I was going to get another chance, but if it did happen I was going to be ready. The opportunity arose to go to USC, and we set out with this vision that we were going to do things better than it's ever been done before.

MASTIN KIPP

When things go wrong and we get uprooted, what if that's not life being against you, or life being harsh? What if those moments are a divine storm? And what if those moments are happening because all the things that don't serve our greatest potential and our spiritual path are being uprooted not to punish you, but for your best interests? What if your worst week or your worst day was divinely sent, and actually your greatest day?

Anastasia Soare was on the brink of releasing her eyebrow product range when her key investor pulled out. Suddenly Anastasia needed $2 million to market, sell, and distribute a warehouse full of her product, and had just seven days to either find the money, or abandon her dream. Rather than quit, Anastasia taught herself everything about the business of marketing, sales, and distribution. Due to her ingenuity and tenaciousness, Anastasia's eyebrow products left the warehouse and went on to become a phenomenal success across the United States and throughout the world.

Michael Acton Smith

I launched this games company, Mind Candy, in 2004, and the first game we created was very creative but it was a commercial disaster. Moshi Monsters was our last roll of the dice, our last chance to build a successful game. We built it, but it used up all the money we had, so at the end of 2008 we basically ran out of cash. My gut instinct was screaming at me that there was some magic here and something really special with this product, but we couldn't find anyone to invest. That period was the biggest obstacle and the craziest time, because I had a team of people that I needed to pay, and we came within a hairsbreadth of having to declare bankruptcy and shut the business down. All those long dark nights, waking up at 4 A.M. in the morning tossing and

turning not knowing how you solve these awful problems.
Luckily I found another angel investor that put in some
money, and just before Christmas we had enough money to
pay the staff salaries and to keep the lights on, and the very
next month we launched our subscription service, and we
have been profitable ever since.

PAUL ORFALEA
The Chinese have a saying: "Crisis is opportunity."
It's a truism that every failure contains the seeds of a
new opportunity.

My dream for *The Secret* film was that it would be released in
every country in the world simultaneously. I had convinced
myself that the only way to do that would be through multiple
television networks across the planet airing it within a 24-hour
period. In the beginning, when the idea of *The Secret* was first
born, international television networks had shown real interest in
the project. However once the film had been completed, without
ever seeing it, one by one the international networks withdrew
their interest. We had completed the film, I was $3 million in debt,
and we had no visible way to release our film to the world.

Then we heard about a company that had created new
technology to stream advertisements on the Internet. A new
possibility to release our film had appeared! Our team worked
frantically with the company to expand the technology to
cater for a full length film, and *The Secret* was released via live

streaming on the Internet – the first film to ever be watched in this way. The technology allowed *The Secret* to be watched across the planet within a 24-hour period, just as I had dreamed.

> "It is better to risk starving to death than surrender. If you give up on your dreams, what's left?"

Jim Carrey
Actor

The truth is, while the Supreme Ordeal might sound scary, you probably won't even realize that's what it is when you face it. When you reach this final challenge you are well prepared. To come this far means you have already realized the powerful abilities within you, and you have everything you need to meet – and to triumph over – the Supreme Ordeal.

Part Four

VICTORY

THE REWARD

The Reward

You will have seen the delirious happiness of sports teams winning championships, and of athletes winning gold medals and breaking world records. Their energy is so potent it sweeps over you; you are filled with exhilaration, and even stirred to tears. Yet our feelings in watching them are nothing compared to what the sports person or athlete is feeling in their moment of victory. For it's only after having taken every step of the journey, having persisted through the challenges and overcoming all the obstacles, that you can know what it truly feels like to experience the ultimate reward of the moment of success.

PETE CARROLL
There was a night before the Oklahoma game in 2005. I'm speaking to my team. Here we are in an undefeated season, playing an undefeated team, and the biggest game in the history of college football. What would be worthy to say at

that night's meeting? I walked in and told them that we had created exactly what we set out to do. We wanted to do this better than it's ever been done before, and we had won a ton of games in a row and now were playing the biggest game you could possibly play. We had bought into the vision, we had worked until we created it, and there was no chance they could beat us. But that wasn't the lesson; the lesson for us was that through setting a course and creating a vision, you can achieve exactly what you want to. And we went out and won the game real big.

PETER BURWASH

I've truly had one of the most wonderful lives possible. Today we're the only survivors of all those original seventeen companies that started out. To now take tennis to 134 countries – the vision has been met.

MICHAEL ACTON SMITH

One of the most exciting points in my career was in early 2009 when we launched our subscription service. The product that we built for free we were now asking parents to pay about £5 a month. Our very small team was crowded around the computer when we put it live, and we sat there watching the screen. Within five minutes we had our first order and made our first £5. We were all hugging each other and jumping up and down. And then before we had a chance to compose ourselves, we had a second order come through, and then a third hit, and then a fourth. We were so overjoyed that mums and dads were prepared to pay for this product that we had poured all of our hearts and souls and energy into. It's such an extraordinary feeling.

LIZ MURRAY

I had this beautiful moment where I got into Harvard and I had the scholarship, and I got a chance to speak with one of the first audiences. I used to say to my friends, "This stuff that's happening feels like a movie. It feels like a book." And then sure enough they made a movie about my journey, and then I wrote a book. It reinforced for me that there is magic in this world.

LAYNE BEACHLEY

It's incredibly rewarding to be able to reflect back on a career and go, "I did that? I can't believe I did that!" Sometimes I still can't relate to the person that I was when I was winning all those world titles. But I am very grateful for it; to be able to have the opportunity to change other people's lives just by following my own dream is incredibly satisfying.

LAIRD HAMILTON

To start with such a big dream and to have it manifest itself into a reality brings joy to my heart. It's like a fairytale. All the challenges, all the failures, all the crashes and injuries and wounded hearts were far beyond worth it. I wouldn't change one instant if it would change where I've arrived.

G. M. Rao

Life has given me more than I have ever dreamed. If I hadn't followed my dream, I would have led an ordinary life.

Anastasia Soare

I have the best life – like a movie. I do what I love. How blessed are you when you do what you love? I enjoyed the journey, and I still enjoy every single day like it's a new day. It's the best feeling to have no regrets at the end of life.

The ultimate reward of the success of your dream does not mark the end of the journey, but the beginning of another. Suddenly, financial rewards and countless opportunities to expand or build on your dream will flood into your life. The money, opportunities, and success bring with them a glorious sense of freedom, but they don't compare with the overwhelming joy and satisfaction that you *did* it – out of nothing, you made something.

Paul Orfalea

Every morning I start by asking what I want to do with this particular day. That's freedom.

Mastin Kipp

I have the freedom to travel and freedom to create and design my life however I want. I'm completely location-independent, so I can run my business from Bali, from Maui, from India, from South Africa, from New York. That freedom is so cool; even though I'm traveling I'm still able to make money and

*run a business. That's just thrilling. And the coolest thing is
I can wake up whenever I want. I used to hate getting up for
school in the morning; it was the worst.*

ANASTASIA SOARE
*The bigger the dream of course the bigger the money is. Any
dream has to have a financial reward.*

When success comes most likely you will find yourself standing
in a place where, perhaps for the first time in your life, you can
buy things you've always wanted to buy, you can travel to places
you've always wanted to go, and you can do things you've
always wanted to do. Along with that, you have the incredible
opportunity to be able to share your success with family and
friends, so that their lives can improve too.

MASTIN KIPP
*There are two things that have been extremely rewarding
– being able to give back, and having the resources to help
other people. I finally am able to give at the level that I've
always wanted to give.*

LIZ MURRAY
*The people I was struggling with when I was homeless are
my family to this day. People I have known now for sixteen,
seventeen years. And when I had a little bit of money I got
so excited because I was able to create experiences for all of
us. We started with our needs: we all went to the dentist.*

A couple of my friends needed rent and an apartment; we took care of the rent. My friend's dad had cancer and needed surgery; we were able to get him the surgery. I was able to have a roof over my head. Being able to take care of the people that I love, being able to contribute something and make people's lives better, brought me tremendous joy. That's been one of the most rewarding experiences in my life.

I was born into quite humble beginnings, and while we didn't have much money, we had each other. I was very fortunate to have been brought up in an environment of safety and security, surrounded by the love of my family. My parents worked really hard all their lives, but they never had much money. When my father died, my mother was not only left without the love of her life, she was also left with little money, and she had no income. My father died before the success of *The Secret,* so he never got to see that dream materialize. But my mother did. She had spent her whole life barely making ends meet, and then after *The Secret,* all of that changed.

I remember one particular day when my mother called me in tears. She had gone into a store and purchased several items of clothing for herself. She was in tears because for the first time in her life she had purchased clothes without having to ask how much they cost.

If you've been lucky enough to have a parent who has dedicated their life to your growth and wellbeing, then you will understand how I felt that day. Nothing I could ever give to my mother would equal what she had given to me in my life.

PETER FOYO

Some people say, "Why do you still work?" And I say, "Because I'm making a difference, and I'd like to continue to do that while I'm here."

Working for the Joy of It

There's no better feeling in the world than to have found your dream and be living it. To work for the sheer joy of it, to wake up and be really excited on a Monday, to love what you do so much that the idea of a long vacation seems boring – that is living!

PETER BURWASH

Back in the late 70s, early 80s, I lived in Hawaii. At 6 o'clock in the morning I'm on the elevator, I've got a 6:30 tennis lesson, and I'm looking around and I'm thinking, "These poor people have to go to work at this hour." I just never really felt like I've gone to a job or done any work at all.

JOHN PAUL DEJORIA

I love what I do. I look forward to going to my office. I look forward to seeing people I work with. I chose this way of life and it's a good one.

PETE CARROLL

I would love to do what I'm doing whether I was getting paid or not. It's interesting that most of our players say the same thing. It's great that we're professionals and we get paid well to do this, but we would do it anyway. You're fortunate to have the opportunity to feel that way about what you do.

MICHAEL ACTON SMITH

A lot of people say, "If I made money, if I was successful in business, I would retire at age thirty." It just so rarely happens, because the people who have that drive and that big dream and vision to build something amazing are not the sort of people who just want to put their feet up and retire.

I was offered a lot of money to sell *The Secret* film, and at the time I was in colossal debt with no visible way to release it to the world. But to sell my dream was inconceivable to me. It would be like selling my greatest joy and reason for living, and there's no amount of money that can ever buy that.

MICHAEL ACTON SMITH

I had opportunities to sell this business for very significant amounts of money – hundreds of millions of dollars – but I don't want to sail off into the sunset and drink cocktails on a yacht. I love what I do. I want to keep building and creating things and working with extraordinary people. That's what gets me out of bed in the morning.

Experiencing the rewards from realizing a dream is glorious, and every person who fulfills their dream deserves each and every one of those rewards. Most likely you will also be filled with excitement and enthusiasm to continue to build on your success and take your dream even further, now knowing that you have the qualities and abilities within you to achieve anything you can think of. But this is not the end of your story. This is not the end of this journey. There's one more vital step that must be taken to complete the Hero's Journey, and it's this final step that causes the transformation – of a human being into a hero.

A LIFE WORTH LIVING

A Life Worth Living

PETER BURWASH

Our body has limits on it as to what we can do to satisfy it. There's a limited amount that we can eat at one time. There's a limit to what we can drink. However, the ability to serve others is unlimited. People who are the happiest in the world are those who are doing things for others.

Something colossal happens to you on your Hero's Journey. You undergo a transformation, and through that transformation you are driven to take one more step on the journey. It's the final step. In taking this final step you become a true hero, and the Hero's Journey is complete.

The fire of passion that you had to realize your dream transforms into a fire of compassion, and you return home, so to speak, to help those who are disadvantaged as you once were. You know their suffering. You know their feeling of hopelessness, because you experienced it. And you are called with the mightiest summoning to do everything you can, to use whatever means you have, to help and inspire as many lives as possible with everything you've acquired on your journey.

MASTIN KIPP

There are two places where a hero gets stuck. The first is when the call to adventure comes, and every hero goes through the phase of the refusal of the call. That's well known. What's not as well known is the refusal of the return, when the hero has claimed their prize and they're in such bliss and such joy they don't want to leave. But the journey is not complete until you take that elixir of life and bring it back to your homeland and share it with others. What makes a hero a hero is that it's not a selfish journey; a hero is someone who's made their life about something more than just themselves.

"When we quit thinking primarily about ourselves and our own self-preservation, we undergo a truly heroic transformation of consciousness."

Joseph Campbell

Mythologist

With all the success and all the rewards you have attained, it is when a vision bigger than yourself takes a grip of your heart that the hero from within emerges. You are compelled to share what has been called "the magic elixir of life" – everything you learned on your journey – so that you will make a difference in the lives of as many people as you can.

PETER BURWASH

Laurance Rockefeller said that you'll know you've matured in life when you understand that the highest position you will ever attain is that of a servant; the person who gets comfortable with that is the person who's really going to have a successful life. And the key to being able to be of service to everybody is to be very, very humble. That's your crown jewel. That's your final achievement in life; it's the most important lesson of them all.

LIZ MURRAY

When I use my life in any way that makes another person's life better, I feel most alive.

G. M. RAO

Society has given me all that I have today, and I feel it is my responsibility to return my gratitude and practice social responsibility as a value.

When you've completed the Hero's Journey, you know that without the support of the people who helped you, you could never have achieved your dream. With the deepest gratitude for all you've received, and the deepest compassion for people who are still struggling, you can't stop yourself from giving back and making a difference in the lives of others. This fire of compassion you feel is so great that no matter what you do, no matter how much you give, you just want to do more.

PETER BURWASH

How important is it for me to make a contribution and do something that matters? It's my life existence. It's why I get up in the morning. It's what allows me to put my head on a pillow at night and feel a tremendous sense of satisfaction.

MICHAEL ACTON SMITH

If you have a lot of money and it's just sitting in a bank doing nothing, that just feels like a waste of potential. You should put it out there doing things. It feels good to help and support people and to see them fulfill their dreams and lead happier lives.

PETER FOYO

When I sit in my office and I see one of the people on my team and I see their children running around the hallway, there is absolutely nothing more gratifying in that moment. To see that child is happy, healthy, is going to a nice school… knowing there's a person you're directly taking care of because of an idea you had one day.

Paul Orfalea

I'm not working my ass off so my boys can live in a fancy mansion. They are going to get enough, and that's it. It's all going to charity and I am going to give it all away before I die.

G. M. Rao

I was fortunate that the Universe gave me the opportunity to serve society. On my part, I have pledged my entire shareholding to the foundation, which we run.

This final step on the Hero's Journey is not about simply writing a check to a charity. It's about finding a way to give your time, energy, and passion in an area that resonates in your heart. It's about finding particular people who are in a similar disadvantaged situation as you were once in, or finding people who are lacking the means to achieve what you've achieved. With all your acquired skills and abilities, you set out to improve other lives in whatever way you can, and provide them with opportunities so they also can follow their dreams.

Anastasia Soare

I went to South Africa when Oprah opened her school there for the girls. I have never seen her so transported, so happy. Her energy was so unbelievable, because she was changing those girls' lives. Giving back is the most fulfilling experience you can have in life. Giving back is the best.

Successful people know that only giving money is not the ultimate answer to help people, and the ones who've completed the journey are very diligent in ensuring that where they give their money provides the means and opportunities for people to change their own life.

JOHN PAUL DEJORIA

Now, my biggest dream is to take an entire country and help it develop and prosper with ecology in mind.

They either choose to give money to provide people with fundamental survival needs, such as clean water, or they use their money to provide people with the means and opportunities they need to live a fulfilling life. It's like the idea in the old saying, to not give fish alone, but also provide the means and skills so people can fish for themselves. It's a principle that will guide you in where to give your money, your time, and any other thing you have to give.

PETE CARROLL

There are millions of causes around the world, and I wish I could help them all, but A Better LA really connected to where we were, right there in Los Angeles. It was all around the area we worked. We deal with people one-on-one and try to help them find hope and realize that if they create visions for themselves, they can really command and control the world that they're in. Fortunately, we have been able to be a factor in saving some families and saving some kids. I feel

*very proud to be connected to it. I wish I could give more
and do more.*

Inspiration, encouragement, and hope are also things you can
give to other people every day, and those things can often do
more for somebody than any amount of money you could give.

Michael Acton Smith

*One of the things I love at the moment is inspiring school
children. They may not even know what entrepreneurship
means, but talking to them and inspiring them, some of them
will go on to create their own businesses and have rewarding,
happy lives down the line.*

From the moment The Secret Company received its first dollar
of revenue, long before it made a profit, the company tithed a
substantial percentage to nonprofit organizations throughout the
world whose work empowers human beings and helps them to
lead fulfilling lives.

Peter Burwash

*We started a wheelchair tennis program, which is now
literally all over the world. We've given free tennis lessons
to every wheelchair player around the world for thirty-eight
years. We've been able to bring a lot of joy and happiness to
people through this sport.*

No matter where you are on your Hero's Journey, or even if you haven't yet embarked upon it, you can give now. When someone needs your help, do whatever you can to help him or her. And there's an important guideline you can follow that will help you know when to help and when not to help: don't do anything that a person can easily do for himself or herself. If you do, you will not help them, but you will disempower them. There's a fine line between helping and disempowering somebody, so help them in ways they cannot easily do for themselves. Inspire them, encourage them, help instill belief in them, and provide them with opportunities so that they can pull themselves out of their current situation. When you do this, you empower them, and there's nothing greater that any one of us can do than to empower another human being with what they need to fulfill their own life.

MASTIN KIPP

No matter what, there is an unlimited opportunity to give. Doesn't matter if you're in a recession, there's still abundant opportunities to give. And when you're great at giving is really when abundance flows to you.

LIZ MURRAY

Sometimes people might think they need to write a book or they need to speak to crowds of thousands. You can be in service in very small ways that are very large in meaning.

PETER FOYO

You can either give people your time or you can give them your resources. We can only enrich our existence the more that we help others.

"If whatever you do helps just one person, you've done something wonderful."

Blake Mycoskie

Founder of TOMS Shoes

JOHN PAUL DEJORIA

When we were six years old, my mother took my brother and me to downtown Los Angeles at Christmas time. While we were there, she gave us ten cents and asked us to walk over and put it in this bucket where a man was ringing a bell. We did, and we asked our mom, "Why did we give that man a dime?" In those days we had very little money, and you could buy two large soda pops and maybe three candy bars with a dime. And our mom said, "That's the Salvation Army. They take care of people who are homeless. Remember this, boys, as long as you live, that no matter how much we have, there's always somebody who has less. Always try and do a little something." That instilled in me to give back no matter what you have, which I think is part of someone becoming successful. A success unshared is failure.

When you give back in whatever way you can, no matter how big or small, the happiness you feel in knowing you have helped another human being will never leave you. In fact, the joy and happiness you feel is so great that it can make you wonder whether the reason you were called to follow your dream was really so that you would reach this final step on the Hero's Journey, where a vision greater than yourself would take over you.

LIZ MURRAY

When you ask people about their dreams and it gets to the bottom line, it's always, "Because I want to make people's lives better." It's a desire we have inside of us that I think we're born with, and it's part of fulfilling our destiny to be here.

LAIRD HAMILTON

I only wish to figure out how to do more and make a bigger difference, and as I continue in that direction I think I may realize, at the end, that my goal was more to make a difference than it was all the other things.

THE HERO IN YOU

The Hero in You

After taking the final step on the Hero's Journey, you become a whole, holy human being – a true hero. Your mind and consciousness that became limited when you undertook the journey on planet Earth have undergone a transformation; where before the circumstances of life seemed to have no rhyme or reason, you can now clearly see that life works in precise and understandable ways. Through your compassion for other people, your mind becomes united with the Universe, who is for all people. As your compassion deepens, confusion, suffering, and fear begin to disappear, and in their place comes an intelligence and knowing that is far beyond the knowledge acquired from reading books and getting degrees. You remember all that you are, you see we are all one family on earth, and you are filled with complete peace and an absolute joy for life. This is your story, and this is your destiny.

I know the potential you have within you. I know the heroic virtues and powers you have within you. This is your story, but only you can live it. This is your Hero's Journey, but only you can take it. You now have the map and the compass, and you have all of us with you, every step of the way.

PETER FOYO

You can have a happier, more fulfilling existence. It's all within you to break out; irrespective of where you are or the circumstances you're in.

LAYNE BEACHLEY

I believe in you, but that amounts to nothing unless you believe in yourself. Believe in yourself, and do everything you can to achieve what you ultimately want in life.

PETE CARROLL

Every person has the power. So often we allow the power to go to people around us who have opinions, or we look at where we come from or what our background is, and we don't give ourselves enough credit that we do have the power to create what we want to. That is the most important message that I could convey to anybody.

G. M. RAO

Believe in your dreams and never let go. Be persistent, keep believing, and it will be realized. Every journey starts with a dream, and your full faith and belief in your dream will pave the way.

John Paul DeJoria

The big difference between successful people and unsuccessful people is the successful ones don't expect anything. Go out there and do it yourself. If you don't succeed, keep on trying until you do. Everyone has that power — you have that power.

Liz Murray

In the end, what we make of this life all comes down to interpretation. It's the story we tell ourselves about who we are and why we're here that determines the quality of our experience. The good news is, you can change that story any time, for you are and always will be the sole author of your life.

Peter Foyo

What can I do, how loud can I yell, for everyone to hear me that you are a hero? Every single human being is a hero. You can be a hero in your own world.

With every step you take, with everything you seek to accomplish in your life, with every dream you want to fulfill, you are seeking eternal happiness. And you will continue to seek that eternal happiness, up every hill and down every dale, until eventually, at the end of the Hero's Journey, you will discover that the eternal happiness you've been looking for is in the discovery of who you really are.

This is the completion of the Hero's Journey for every one of us here on planet Earth. Only you can take the greatest journey of discovery. Only you can discover the truth about who you really are; only you can discover the hero within you. Until that time, every day of your life, throughout the eons, the hero within you will continue to call.

Featured in Hero

Through revenue received from this book, The Secret Company is honored to contribute to the following foundations and charities of *Hero*'s contributors.

MICHAEL ACTON SMITH
www.mindcandy.com

Michael Acton Smith is the CEO and creative director of Mind Candy, the kids' entertainment company behind the global phenomenon, Moshi Monsters. Moshi Monsters is an online game and virtual world, but also includes toys, trading cards, magazines, a book, and a movie. Michael continues to lead Mind Candy with his vision of building the greatest Entertainment Company for the digital generation.

THE MOSHI FOUNDATION
www.themoshifoundation.com

Michael established **The Moshi Foundation** as a grant-giving organization to assist children and young people throughout the world. To date, grants have been provided to support advances in education, health and welfare, to overcome financial hardship, and to assist in therapy and education for children with special needs and disabilities.

LAYNE BEACHLEY
www.laynebeachley.com

 Layne Beachley is the most successful competitive female surfer in history, and winner of a record seven world titles. She is currently vice president of the International Surfing Association, and sits on the board of Surfing Australia and the Sport Australia Hall of Fame. Layne continues to surf every day, occasionally competes in master's events, and is a motivational speaker.

LAYNE BEACHLEY AIM FOR THE STARS FOUNDATION
www.aimforthestars.com.au

Layne established the **Layne Beachley Aim for the Stars Foundation** with the goal to provide financial support and encouragement to young women and girls to help them realize their dreams. The program is open to dedicated females throughout Australia in the fields of sports, academia, or community and cultural pursuits. Layne's aim is to help these young women and girls in their quest to achieve greatness.

Peter Burwash

www.peterburwash.com

 Peter Burwash is a former professional tennis player and one of the most revered tennis coaches of all time. Peter is founder and president of the world's largest tennis management company, Peter Burwash International, providing top-level tennis coaching and individual programs in thirty-two countries around the world. Peter is also a bestselling author and in-demand motivational speaker.

Care For Vrindavan

www.fflvrindavan.org

As a result of his international travels, Peter has come to support the **Care For Vrindavan** organization, a US-based charity that raises funds on behalf of the impoverished Vrindavan region of India. Local communities are provided with basic necessities, enabling them to build self-reliance for the future. Specifically, this charity funds the education of thousands of otherwise neglected Indian girls, so that they may reach their full potential.

PETE CARROLL
www.petecarroll.com

 Pete Carroll is an American football coach and winner of two national championships, along with multiple conference and divisional titles. Pete is currently head coach and executive vice president of the Seattle Seahawks, where he was recently awarded NFC Coach of the Year.

A BETTER LA AND A BETTER SEATTLE
www.abetterla.org
www.abetterseattle.com

Pete is renowned for his philanthropic work, particularly for his efforts to reduce gang and youth violence in Los Angeles and Seattle. Pete established **A Better LA** and **A Better Seattle**, which aim to empower individuals to create safer and stronger communities. These organizations partner with community-based organizations to provide families and youth with the tools, mentorship, and support to help them thrive.

JOHN PAUL DEJORIA

www.paulmitchell.com

John Paul DeJoria is a businessman who cofounded John Paul Mitchell Systems, creator of hair care products and beauty schools. John Paul is the company CEO, and has achieved annual turnover in excess of $1 billion. In 1989, he cofounded and now owns the majority of the Patrón Spirits Company. John Paul is also passionate about environmental issues, international diplomacy, and philanthropy.

JP's PEACE, LOVE & HAPPINESS FOUNDATION

www.peacelovehappinessfoundation.org

Having spent time in the foster care system as a child and endured stints of homelessness as an adult, John Paul has dedicated substantial resources to his charity, **JP's Peace, Love & Happiness Foundation**. The organization supports environmental sustainability, social responsibility, and the protection of animals, and aims to enable people to help themselves through gardening and farming programs that equip them to feed their families and start their own businesses.

PETER FOYO

www.nextel.com.mx

Peter Foyo is a business executive and international telecommunications expert. Peter is regarded as one of the very best and most innovative CEOs throughout Latin America. He serves on the board of several companies and continues to lead a 17,000-strong workforce as president of Nextel Communications Mexico.

NEXTEL FOUNDATION

www.nextel.com.mx/nextelfundacion.html

As company CEO, Peter has built an admirable culture of corporate social responsibility and philanthropy. The **Nextel Foundation** provides support for the most vulnerable members of the community through education. The foundation supports students through scholarships and programs aimed at youth, the underprivileged, and the disabled, and by funding scientific research and higher education.

LAIRD HAMILTON
www.lairdhamilton.com

 Laird Hamilton is a world-renowned big-wave surfer, innovator, and pioneer of tow-in surfing, stand-up paddle boarding, and hydrofoil surfing. Laird continues to split his time between riding the big waves, developing new forms of crossover surf sports, and raising awareness for causes close to his heart.

RAINCATCHER
www.raincatcher.org/laird

Laird and his wife, Gabrielle Reece, were recently appointed to the board of directors of **RainCatcher**, a nonprofit organization established to alleviate the global water crisis. RainCatcher has assisted 700,000 people worldwide through the provision of rainwater-harvesting systems. RainCatcher aims to provide clean drinking water to an additional 10 million people by 2015.

MASTIN KIPP

www.thedailylove.com

Mastin Kipp is an entrepreneur, writer, and blogger, who utilizes social media to spread his messages of inspiration. Mastin founded *The Daily Love*, a website, daily email, and Twitter account, which reaches 600,000 subscribers a day, and is syndicated through *The Huffington Post*. Mastin has made appearances on *Oprah's Lifeclass*, and has been featured by Oprah on her *Super Soul Sunday* as a next-generation spiritual thinker.

ANTHONY ROBBINS FOUNDATION

www.anthonyrobbinsfoundation.org

Mastin credits his transformation to the help of Life Coach Anthony Robbins, and in gratitude, he has lent his support to the **Anthony Robbins Foundation**. This nonprofit organization conducts programs designed to aid and enrich the lives of those most often forgotten by society: youth, the elderly, the homeless, and the prison population.

Liz Murray

www.homelesstoharvard.com

Liz Murray is a bestselling author and one of the most highly sought-after motivational speakers in the world, famous for her incredible journey from homelessness to attending Harvard University. She has shared the stage with the likes of Mikhail Gorbachev, the Dalai Lama, and Tony Blair, and has been honored by the White House as well as Oprah Winfrey for her inspirational work in empowering the young.

Momentum Teens for Leadership

www.momentumteens.org

As a role model for teenagers, Liz is proud to support **Momentum Teens for Leadership**, a not-for-profit organization whose aim is to encourage, empower, and nurture leadership skills among youth. Momentum Teens offers workshops and programs that provide tools and experiences to help teens become responsible, confident contributors to their community and the world.

Paul Orfalea
www.paulorfalea.com

 Paul Orfalea is the founder of Kinko's, the world's leading office supplies and business services chain. Having divested his interest in Kinko's, Paul spreads his time between passing on his knowledge and experience as a university professor, and his various philanthropic interests.

Orfalea Foundation
www.orfaleafoundation.org

Under Paul's leadership, the **Orfalea Foundation** has endeavored to empower others to find their own strengths. Supported programs include innovative early-childhood education, high school programs for motivated students, thousands of higher-education scholarships, and substantial funding for select university programs. Paul is also dedicated to assisting the plight of single parents, and ensuring healthy school food for children.

G. M. RAO
www.gmrgroup.in

G. M. Rao is the founder and chairman of GMR Group, a global energy and infrastructure development corporation based in Bangalore, India. A visionary business leader, Mr. Rao has more recently steered his company toward urban development and the creation of national assets, such as power plants, highways, and airports.

GMR VARALAKSHMI FOUNDATION
www.gmrgroup.in/foundation.html

Mr. Rao is a strong advocate of corporate social responsibility, and established the **GMR Varalakshmi Foundation** to address the lack of basic amenities and abject poverty within local communities. The foundation seeks to make quality education available to everyone. Health needs are addressed through the provision of hospitals, medical clinics, and ambulances. Self-employment opportunities are created through the establishment of training institutes and entrepreneurial programs for enterprising youth.

ANASTASIA SOARE
www.anastasia.net

 Anastasia Soare is considered to be the definitive eyebrow expert, and is a beauty industry icon. Due to her unique eyebrow shaping method, Anastasia has built an enviable clientele comprising the who's who of Hollywood, and maintains flagship salons in Beverly Hills and Brentwood. There are also Anastasia brow studios in high-end department stores worldwide, and she has personally developed and released a range of exclusive eyebrow and makeup products.

ANASTASIA BRIGHTER HORIZON FOUNDATION
www.anastasiafoundation.org

Through the **Anastasia Brighter Horizon Foundation**, young adults emerging from the foster-care system are offered scholarships to pursue careers in beauty and skincare. Funding and support is provided to assist with beauty school education, internships, hands-on training, and job placement. The aim is to create self-sufficiency and a foundation for the future.

Further Reading
from Hero's Contributors

LAYNE BEACHLEY
Beneath the Waves
Layne Beachley's testimony to the power of self-belief.
Publisher: Random House Australia, 2009

PETER BURWASH
Becoming the Master of Your D-A-S-H
Personal anecdotes, realizations, and sage advice from enlightened people, past and present, providing fundamental guidelines for improving our life journey.
Publisher: Torchlight Publishing, 2007

Dear Teenager
Peter Burwash provides an invaluable guide to teenagers for growing up healthy and whole physically, mentally, and spiritually.
Publisher: Torchlight Publishing, 2008

LAIRD HAMILTON
Force of Nature: Mind, Body, Soul, And, of Course, Surfing
Laird Hamilton shares his unique philosophy that he used to become one of the greatest big-wave surfers the world has seen.
Publisher: Rodale Books, 2008

MASTIN KIPP

Daily Love
Publisher: Hay House Publishing, release date 2014

LIZ MURRAY

Breaking Night: A Memoir of Forgiveness, Survival, and My Journey from Homeless to Harvard
Liz Murray's inspirational story, from living on the streets to graduating from Harvard University.
Publisher: Hyperion, 2010

PAUL ORFALEA

Copy This!: Lessons from a Hyperactive Dyslexic who Turned a Bright Idea into One of America's Best Companies
Paul Orfalea's story of being a struggling kid who could barely read or write, to creating Kinko's and building it into a $1.5 billion empire.
Publisher: Workman Publishing Co., Inc., New York
© The Orfalea Family Foundation 2005

www.thesecret.tv